AA

50 Walks to COUNTRY PUBS

Produced by AA Publishing

Compiled by Ann F Stonehouse

Published by AA Publishing (a trading name of Automobile Association Developments Limited, whose registered office is Millstream, Maidenhead, Windsor, SL4 5GD; registered number 1878835)

ISBN 0 7495 3972 0

A01835

A CIP catalogue record for this book is available from the British Library.

The contents of this book are believed correct at the time of printing. Nevertheless, the publishers cannot be held responsible for any errors or omissions or for changes in the details given in this book or for the consequences of any reliance on the information it provides. We have tried to ensure accuracy, but things do change and we would be grateful if readers would advise us of any inaccuracies they encounter. This does not affect your statutory rights.

We have taken all reasonable steps to ensure that these walks are safe and achievable by walkers with a realistic level of fitness. However, all outdoor activities involve a degree of risk and the publishers accept no responsibility for any injuries caused to readers whilst following these walks. For more advice on walking safely see page 127. The mileage range shown on the cover is for guidance only – some walks may exceed or be less than these distances.

These routes may appear in the AA's *50, 100 Local Walks* series and *The Pub Guide 2004*

Visit AA Publishing at ***www.theAA.com***

Printed and bound by Scotprint, Scotland

Walking for Pleasure

Whether it's a Sunday stroll or a serious hike, there's nothing to beat a good walk in the countryside. And when you can combine the virtues of a healthy walk in the great outdoors with a spot of indulgence in a really good pub – before, after or even during the walk – then surely life doesn't get much better!

For this collection we've chosen walks across the length and breadth of England, Scotland and Wales, based around 50 of the best pubs in the AA's annually updated *Pub Guide*. The AA's *Pub Guide* includes information about hundreds of pubs, selected for their atmosphere, good food and beer (check out more on the AA's internet site, ***www.theAA.com***).

Each pub in this book was highlighted in the recent 'Pick of the Pubs' selection, and many have supplied their own suggestion for a great walk near by. All of them serve good food, using fresh local ingredients, and some of them offer accommodation if you're planning a longer break.

All the walks will take you into attractive areas of countryside. They range from 2 to 10 miles (1.6–16km) in length, but average out at 4–5 miles (6.4–8km), with lots of options for extra loops and extensions, and even one train ride. We've supplied maps to help you find your way around 30 of the routes, but wherever you're walking we recommend that you take the relevant Ordnance Survey map with you as well.

Please check out the safety notes on page 127 before you set out, and remember to park your car courteously – patrons are usually welcome to leave it in the pub car park if they ask first.

Enjoy your walking!

The best way to see Britain is on foot

Locator map

The country is divided up into regions and the colour of each region corresponds with the colour band at the top of the page through the book. The location of each walk is marked with a black dot and a number, e.g. **16: A short hike around historic Hever page 45**

Contents

Contents

How to use this book

The fifty routes with their recommended pubs are organised through the book by region, and then by county within that region. Locate them via the map on page 4, or browse through the contents listings for the walk of your choice. All the routes except one are circular.

Walks

Near the start of each walk there is a green information panel. This gives the approximate distance of the walk in both miles and kilometres, plus the distance of any optional extension walk. It also lists the relevant Ordnance Survey map which you will need, and the start and finish point of the walk, including a grid reference to help you locate it on the OS map.

Start points include information on suitable car parking where that information is available. Where the start point is also the location of a pub, **please ask in advance if you want to leave your car in the pub's own private car park**.

A number in the 'ascent/gradient' category gives a broad indication of whether the terrain is level (1) or notably steep in parts (3). 'Paths' outlines the sort of tracks you'll be on, including an indication of the stiles you'll encounter, and 'Landscape' gives a quick picture of the sort of countryside you'll be walking through.

Where appropriate, numbers in the walk instructions correspond to numbers on the given map, where the route is marked in a broken red line. Letters are used in a similar way for extension walks, which are marked with a dotted red line.

Pubs

Information about the recommended pub for each walk appears alongside the walking instructions in a tinted panel. The name of the pub is followed by its address and phone number, and directions to help you find the pub if you are heading there first. Under the pub's opening times are given the times when food is served in the bar and/or restaurant, with a broad indication of average prices. Note that last orders may be 30 minutes before the times stated, and these details may change at short notice – so if you're counting on it, ring the pub and check ahead.

For beer fans we've listed the pub's brewery or company where appropriate, along with a short selection of the principal beers available – there may be many more when you get there! 'Free house' means that the pub is independently owned and run.

Below this, we have listed some of the facilities available, such as which pubs welcome children and dogs, how much parking is available, and which pubs offer accommodation, with a starting price guide. Breakfast is generally included in the price, but guests should check ahead when making a reservation.

Credit cards are widely accepted, but in a small number of cases we have highlighted where this is not so.

Pub opening hours:

Pubs in England and Wales are permitted to open and sell alcohol from 11am–11pm on Mondays to Saturdays. On Sundays, licensing hours are noon–10.30. You must be 18 years old or over to buy and consume alcohol in a bar. Children under 14 are allowed into pubs holding a Children's Certificate. They must be accompanied by an adult and are restricted to those areas certified suitable for young children.

In Scotland pubs and clubs can be open for the sale of alcohol from 11am–11pm on Mondays to Saturdays, and 12.30–2.30 and 6.30–11 on Sundays (the afternoon gap may be bridged by a regular extension). Occasional or regular extensions to permitted hours may allow premises to open late. **Note:** many pubs close on Christmas Day, and some on 1 January.

1: A ramble on the Cornish coast

Enjoy a walk with breath-taking views along the beach and cliffs of the south Cornish shore.

Walk information

Distance: 3 miles (4.8km)
Map: OS Explorer 103 The Lizard, Falmouth & Helston
Start/finish: Halzephron Inn; grid ref SX 657224
Ascent/gradient: 2
Paths: steep coastal cliff path, tarmac road
Landscape: dramatic coastline of south Cornwall

Blue seas at Gunwalloe Cove

Walk directions

❶ From the **Halzephron Inn,** cross the road and go down the lane towards a cove. From here there are glorious views along the shingle beach to Mousehole and Land's End. Turn left along the track, then head up steeply towards Halzephron Herb Farm.

❷ Follow the path round to the right and along the impressive cliffs, notoriously the scene of many shipwrecks over the centuries. Look out along here for kittiwakes, cormorants, gulls and lapwings.

❸ Continue round to Gwinian Head. At this point you begin to drop down gently to Dollar Cove, named after a Spanish galleon wrecked on the cliffs below in 1785 with a cargo of 2½ tons of gold coins. Gold doubloons and other coins have been found on the beach. While here, have a look at

the beautiful 13th-century church of St Winwaloe. The decorated panels inside were originally part of a 16th-century rood screen made from a ship, the *St Anthony*, wrecked in 1526 en route to Portugal from Flanders. The golden sands of Church Cove with Mullion golf links behind them and Poldhu cliffs across the bay – setting for Marconi's wireless station – make a memorable scene.

❹ Take the road up the hill, following it between traditional Cornish hedges filled with wild flowers and birds, and make for a magnificent view across Mount's Bay at the top. Head back down the hill to return to the inn.

Halzephron Inn

Gunwalloe TR12 7QB
Tel: 01326 240406
Directions: *3 miles (4.8km) south of Helston on A3083, turn right to Gunwalloe; go through the village; inn on the left overlooking Mount's Bay*
Open: *11–2.30, 6.30–11 (summer 6–11)*
Bar meals: *lunch and dinner served all week, 12–2, 7–9*
Restaurant: *lunch and dinner served all week, 12–2, 7–9*
Brewery/company: *free house*
Principal beers: *Sharp's Own, Doom Bar & Coaster, St Austell Tribute, Halzephron Gold*
Children welcome
Parking: *14*

Quintessentially Cornish, this *500-year-old free house is spectacularly situated on the South-West Coast footpath, overlooking Mount's Bay. Formerly known as the Ship, the pub was 'dry' for half a century until 1956, when its licence was restored. Its unusual name comes from the old Cornish Als Yfferin, or 'Cliffs of Hell', a name borne out by the numerous wrecks along this rugged coast.*

A shaft still connects the pub to an underground tunnel, which was used by smugglers. They included the local hero Henry Cuttance, who was also a landlord and a notable wrestler. Modern visitors will find a warm welcome, with real ales and a fine selection of malt whiskies.

The menu changes twice daily and is based on freshly prepared local produce. Options range from lunchtime sandwiches to evening specials such as crab bisque with Welsh rarebit croutons, straw potato and candied lemon, and peppered venison fillet on spinach with potato fondant, celeriac purée and bramble jus.

Walk information

Distance: 5 miles (8km) + extension 2 miles (3.2km)
Map: OS Explorer 103 The Lizard
Start/finish: large car park at Helford; grid ref SW 759261
Ascent/gradient: 2
Paths: good woodland paths and tracks and field paths; short section of quiet lane; 10 stiles
Landscape: wooded creekside and fields
Note: only authorised cars are allowed beyond the car park into Helford village

Small sailing craft dot the Helford river

2: Exploring the tidal creeks of Helford

The Helford River is enduringly popular with land-based visitors and leisure sailors alike, yet the area manages somehow to absorb it all.

Cars probe tentatively between the unforgiving stone hedges of narrow Cornish lanes. The bulk of river craft are yachts, so that on a busy sailing day you will hear only the pleasing flap of sails blowing through, as flocks of vessels tack across the estuary mouth. The pelt of trees that lines the estuary and its subsidiary creeks plays a great part in this muffling of too much human racket.

Yet the picturesque, leisure-dominated Helford of today was once a bustling haven for all sorts of trade, and not least, was a haven for pirates and smugglers. During Elizabethan times especially, a passel of Cornish rascals, from the highest in the land to the lowest, was engaged in plundering the cargoes of vessels that sailed through the Channel approaches. The Helford, as it is popularly known, was a secretive, useful base from which all manner of goods could be spirited away inland. In later times the river became an equally secretive base for missions against German-occupied France during World War II.

There is little physical evidence of any of this busy past, but in the shrouded creeks that run off like fibrous roots from the main river it is easy to imagine the utter remoteness of life hundreds of years ago, when movement by sea was far more convenient than by land.

This walk starts from the village of Helford and follows the southern shore of the estuary between Treath and Dennis Head, mainly through the deep woodland of the Bosahan estate. There are tantalising glimpses of the river through the trees and the path skirts tiny coves such as Bosahan and Ponsence with their inviting beaches that must surely have seen their share of night-landings in the piratical past.

The return leg of the walk follows the north shore of the adjacent Gillan Creek, far smaller and thus far less accommodating to vessels than the deep Helford. Here the tiny Church of St Anthony adds to the overall serenity. From near the head of the creek, you climb inland to Manaccan, a charming hamlet that seems to tumble down the slopes of the valley. Beyond the village the route leads into

Look for

There are not one but two interesting churches on the route: St Anthony-in-Meneage and St Manacca at Manaccan. At St Anthony the piers of the single aisle lean engagingly to port; the 15th-century font has fine reliefs of angels holding shields. Look for the granite drinking bowl, complete with engaging inscription, outside the main door. Manaccan's church has a splendid south door. Look out for an ancient fig tree that grows out of the wall.

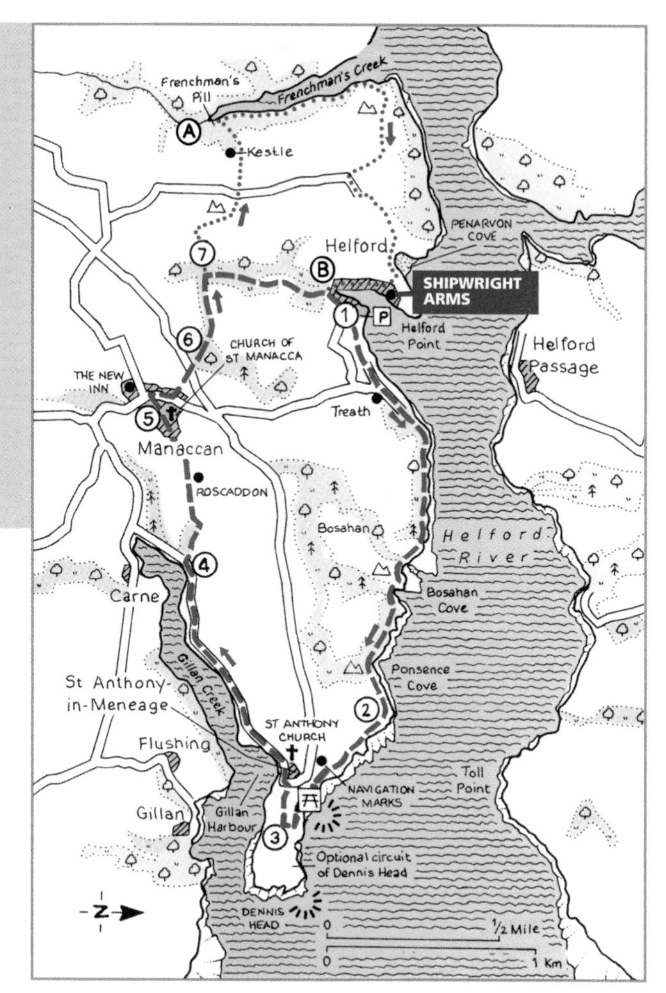

the wooded valley above Helford and takes you back to your starting point. From here, it's a short stroll to the appealing **Shipwright Arms.**

Walk directions

❶ As you leave the car park, turn left along a path, signed 'Coast Path'. Go through a metal gate and follow a sunken track. Descend steps, then turn right along a lane. At a steep right-hand bend, bear off ahead along a track. Follow this permissive path trough trees, keeping left at any junctions.

❷ Leave the wooded area via a metal gate, then turn left along a field edge to a stone stile. Follow the bottom edge of the next two fields. Cross a fence at a field gap beside a white pole and a red post and triangle (these are navigation marks). Follow the field edge ahead. Go through a kissing gate, then follow the field edge (there's a seat and viewpoint on the left), to where it ends at the beginning of a wide track (to make the short circuit of Dennis head, follow the tack ahead to a stile on the left).

❸ To continue on the main route, turn sharply right at the start of the wide track and follow the left-hand field edge and then a path across the open field. Join a track behind a house, then go through a kissing gate and descend to St Anthony's Church. Follow the road alongside Gillan Creek.

❹ Just past where the road curves round a bay, go up right between granite gate posts by a public footpath sign. Follow a broad track through trees to houses at Roscadden. Keep ahead along a track that leads to Manaccan at a T-junction opposite Manaccan Church.

Shipwright Arms

Helford TR12 6JX
Tel: 01326 231235
Directions: *take the A390 through Truro, then A394 to Helston; before Goonhilly Down turn left for Helford and Manaccan*
Open: *11–2.30, 6–11 (closed Sun & Mon nights in winter)*
Bar meals: *lunch and dinner served all week, 12–2, 7–9; average main course £4.75*
Restaurant: *lunch served Sunday only, 12–2; dinner Tue–Sat, 7–9*
Brewery/company: *free house*
Principle beers: *Castle Eden, Greene King IPA, Sharps Doombar*
Children welcome
Dogs allowed

Superbly situated on *the banks of the Helford River in an idyllic village, this small thatched pub is especially popular in summer when customers relax on the three terraces, complete with palm trees and glorious flowers, which lead down to the water's edge. Inside, there's a nautical theme to the pub's décor.*

The summer buffet offers crab and lobster subject to availability, alongside various ploughman's lunches, salads, home-made pies, steaks and a wide range of international dishes.

Look out for the summer barbecues which are held on the terrace.

While there

At the green heart of the Helford River lies the impossibly romantic Frenchman's Creek, which is explored on the extension route. More properly known as Frenchman's Pill, this thin finger of tidal water has become famous through its association with the romantic novel *Frenchman's Creek*, by Daphne du Maurier; but the writer Arthur Quiller Couch had written a short story with the same title long before du Maurier's novel appeared and the source of the name is not certain. It was recorded on 19th-century maps and may yet prove to be a corruption of an old usage, or simply a longstanding reference to French ships that must, at one time, have visited the Helford quite regularly.

❺ Go through the churchyard and on through the gate opposite to a road (the village shop is to the left). Keep ahead to a junction, then go up right, past the school. Keep uphill, then turn left along Minster Meadow, go over a stile, and through two fields to reach a road.

❻ Go diagonally left to the stile opposite, cross a field, then go left following signposts to reach woods. Follow the path ahead. At a junction keep ahead, go over a stile and reach a second junction. (The extended walk starts here.)

❼ Bear down right and follow a broad track through trees to reach some buildings at Helford. Keep ahead on reaching a surfaced road and follow the road uphill to the car park.

Extension to Penarvon

The extension to the main walk maintains the theme of woods and water. It begins at Point ❻, where, instead of bearing down right at the junction, you keep straight on through the trees to reach a field. Turn right along the field edge to a gate and then follow the right edge of the next field to another gate onto a track and then on past Kestle farmhouse to a surfaced road. Cross the road, then cross a field to a track that leads down to join a public footpath signposted 'Footpath along Frenchman's Creek' at Point Ⓐ.

The creek is shrouded by trees, but get your tide and timing right and the water gleams through the tangled branches and flickering leaves. The path leads down the east bank of the creek then climbs to a field. Go right where the track forks, signposted 'Helford via Penarvon Cove'. Just beyond a gate and a cattle grid, turn left down a lane, then fork right to reach Penarvon Cove. From the top end of the beach follow a path that leads to a concrete track, where a left turn takes you down past the **Shipwright Arms** and on through Helford village to join the final part of the main walk at Point Ⓑ.

3: Around picturesque Broadhembury

Broadhembury is one of those unspoilt showpiece Devon villages that gives you the impression that nothing has changed for centuries and that you've entered some sort of time warp.

Walk information

Distance: 5½ miles (9km) + extension 2¾ miles (4.4km)
Map: OS Explorer 115 Exeter & Sidmouth
Start/finish: unsurfaced car park at Knowles Wood; grid ref SY 095068
Ascent/gradient: 2
Paths: country lanes, pastures and woodland paths; 7 stiles
Landscape: rolling farmland and beech woods

The picturesque main street is lined with well-preserved cob and thatched cottages and pretty flower-filled gardens, and there appears to be a constant cycle of repair and renovation going on. Much of Broadhembury as you see it today developed as an estate village under the patronage of the Drewe family in the early 17th century, and this is reflected in the name of the pub, the **Drewe Arms.**

St Andrew's Church holds many memorials to members of the family, who have been highly influential in the development of the village. In 1603 Edward Drewe, Sergeant-at-Law to Queen Elizabeth I, bought Abbey Farm from Dunkeswell Abbey, and created a new mansion, the Grange, which remained the family seat for nearly 300 years. Edward Drewe was a successful lawyer, who already owned Sharpham and Killerton. The oak drawing room at the Grange is said to be one of the most beautiful in the country. The house is not open to the public, but you can get a good view of it from the south-east approach road to the village.

The church was consecrated in 1259, but the building dates mainly from the 15th century, constructed of local flint and chalky limestone from Beer. It's set at the end of a cul-de-sac of chestnut trees and has been much restored over the last couple of centuries. The tower (from about 1480) is almost 100 feet (30m) high. The timbers of the roof were painted in the late 15th century, and were only discovered in 1930 when repair work was being carried out. There is also an unusual 15th-century font which is somewhat damaged (probably during the Civil War) and decorated with primitive figures of apostles and clergy, and an 18th-century memorial to Augustus Toplady, who wrote the hymn 'Rock of Ages'.

Just a mile (1.6km) to the south-east of the village lies Hembury hillfort, on a spur of the Blackdown Hills at 883 feet (269m) above sea level. There was a causewayed camp here around 2500 BC, and in about 150BC Iron Age dwellers built the defensive earthworks that can be seen today. The site was inhabited until around AD 75. In May the ramparts are smothered with a carpet of bluebells.

Walk directions

❶ Return to the road and turn left uphill. Very shortly a bridleway sign points right through another parking area. After a few minutes this narrow, level path reaches a signpost and metal gate (left), indicating that you have reached the Devon & Somerset Gliding Club. Ignore the gate, continue on the bridleway.

❷ Pass through the next metal gate onto the airfield. Turn left along the edge, keeping to the right of the clubhouse. Follow the tarmac drive left over a cattle grid and down the lane to join a road.

❸ Turn right; pass Barleycombe Farm (on the left), then follow bridleway signs right through a gate, left through another and into a field. Follow the track along the bottom of the field. The path curves right through a stand of beech trees and a metal gate, then runs straight across the next field towards a big beech tree and gate. Take the stony track through the gate. After 100 yards (91m) bear right along a grassy path (ignore the gate straight ahead) and through two metal gates, with a coniferous plantation to the right.

❹ The path ends at a lane; turn right downhill into Broadhembury. At St Andrew's

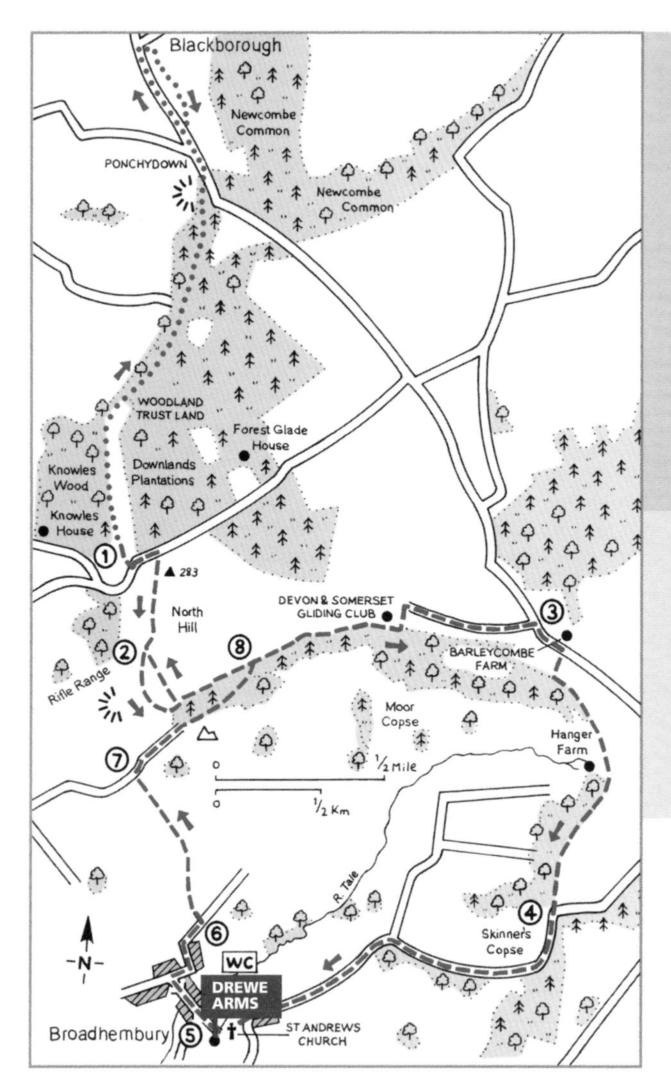

Look for

The Devon & Somerset Gliding Club is near the start of the walk at Northill, over 900 feet (280m) above sea level – a popular spot with skylarks, too! The return leg skirts along the edge of the airfield; the gliders are launched using a steel cable, so it's wise to keep well out of the way. There's something quite magical – and tempting – about watching the gliders drift silently through the air above you, often reaching heights of over 2,000 feet (600m).

While there

Visit Broadhembury Craft Centre, which you will pass as you walk downhill towards the village after Point ❹. Open seven days a week and situated in an attractive courtyard setting, here you will find a range of rural craft workshops.

Church cross the road and go through the churchyard, then under the lychgate and downhill to find the **Drewe Arms** (left) for a welcome break.

❺ To continue the walk, from the pub, turn left down the main street to reach the bridge and ford. Turn right up the lane, past the playground and up the hill.

❻ Just past two thatched cottages go left over the stile in the hedge and up the field, aiming for a stile in the top left corner. Go over that and straight ahead, keeping the old farmhouse and barn conversions to your right. Over the next stile; then another; then right, round the edge of the field, and over a small stile ahead into a small copse. Another stile leads into the next field; look straight across to locate the next stile in the beech hedge opposite, which takes you into a green lane.

❼ Turn right and walk uphill between conifers, on the left, and fields until a metal gate leads on to an open gateway and back on to the airfield.

❽ Turn left along the edge of the field. Go left over the second iron gate to rejoin the bridleway which leads back to the road. Turn left downhill to find your car.

Extension to Blackborough

If you feel like a more relaxing alternative, which will teach you something about local industry in the rural heart of Devon, have a look at the nearby village of Blackborough. You can always add it to the end of the Broadhembury walk if you want to get a more balanced view of the history of the Blackdown Hills.

Leave the car park through the gate opposite the entrance and walk along a broad bridleway, lined with rhododendrons, through Woodland Trust land. This lovely track, with views east over the rolling mid-Devon landscape, leads to a junction of tracks (muddy in wet weather). Keep straight on along the bridleway to meet a lane under beech trees.

Turn left downhill past pretty cottages to reach Ponchydown. Go straight on past the phone box to reach the 'centre' of Blackborough. This whole area feels forgotten, but a notice board tells you that this remote village was the centre of a flourishing whetstone industry in the 18th and 19th centuries. Whetstones (or 'batts') were used to sharpen scythes and sickles for cereal harvesting, and were exported to London and even abroad. The invention of carborundum killed the industry, and by 1900 only three mines remained. This is a fascinating place – ahead you will see old iron gates leading to the overgrown churchyard (a haven for wildlife). The church, which had fallen into disrepair, was demolished in 1994. To the north-west lies the Italianate Blackborough House (built in 1838), which was never completed, and which has gained a reputation as a folly.

You can take a slightly different route back to your car by turning right by the notice board and following the footpath sign uphill towards the woods, then almost immediately right again. This leads back to the lane near the bridleway which you follow back to your car.

Drewe Arms

Broadhembury EX14 3NF
Tel: 01404 841267
Directions: *on A373 halfway between Cullompton and Honiton*
Open: *11–3, 6–11 (Sun 12–3 only)*
Bar meals: *lunch served all week, 12–2; dinner served Mon–Sat, 7–10; average main course £10.50*
Restaurant: *lunch served all week, 12–2; dinner served Mon–Sat, 7–10; average 3 course à la carte £27*
Brewery/company: *free house*
Principal beers: *Otter Ale, Otter Bitter, Otter Head, Otter Bright*
Children welcome
Dogs allowed

Set in an *archetypal thatched Devon village in unspoiled countryside handy for Dartmoor and the spectacular Devon coast, its mullioned windows and quaint old furniture lend the Tudor Drewe Arms its particularly gracious character.*

The best available West Country produce forms the basis of the daily menus, with an emphasis on fresh fish. Expect on any one day to feast on pollack baked with Cheddar and cream, or sea bream with orange and chilli. Steamed mussels with garlic and herbs, griddled sardines and smoked haddock and Stilton rarebit are all offered in two portion sizes – large and very large. Alongside seared scallops with rouille and turbot fillet with hollandaise, on the fixed-price dining menu might be venison tenderloin with wild mushroom sauce, followed by chocolate St Emilion. Dedicated meat-eaters can enjoy rare beef and hot chicken baguettes, and a Bookmaker's fillet steak with anchovy butter. Good house wines from around the world are all offered by the glass. Outdoor eating on the patio.

4: A short hike on Dartmoor

This attractive walk serves as an introduction to the wild and varied beauty of Dartmoor, one of Britain's most popular national parks.

Walk directions

❶ Leave the **Peter Tavy Inn** and follow the lane back towards the centre of the village. Look for a path on the left, running along beside the churchyard wall. After passing the village cross, go along the short track in front of two cottages to join the road.

❷ Turn left up the hill and then take the first lane on the right, leading out to Dartmoor. On reaching the foot of Smeardon Down, take a broad, green path to the left, just beyond the moor gate, and keep to the upper path at a fork. Continue ahead and, with a drystone wall ahead, turn right and begin a fairly long and gradual climb, all the way to Boulter's Tor.

❸ Keep following the line of the wall to reach a wooden five-barred gate and turn right. Cross open ground between a wall on the left and stone markers on the right to reach a rough track. Follow it downhill for about 200 yards (183m) and turn left at the wall corner.

Walk information

Distance: 3 miles (5km)
Map: OS Outdoor Leisure 28 Dartmoor
Start/finish: Peter Tavy Inn; grid ref SX 512778
Ascent/gradient: 2
Paths: paths, tracks and lanes; 1 stile
Landscape: moorland

The pleasant market town of Tavistock

❹ Cross the road to Lower Godsworthy Farm and aim for a fingerpost and wooden five-barred gate below. Enter a field, keeping a line of trees and a hedgerow on the left before crossing open ground to a marker post and a wall stile. A twisty and uneven path descends through Peter Tavy Combe to reach a junction of paths.

❺ Take the path ahead, passing through a metal gate. The path broadens out and passes beside a row of cottages, dropping downhill to reach Higher Mill. Cross the bridge over the Colly Brook and veer right at the fork, following the rough path beside the stream. Reaching the village 'square', take the road round to the right for a short distance before turning left. Return to the **Peter Tavy Inn.**

Peter Tavy Inn

Peter Tavy PL19 9NN
Tel: 01822 810348
Directions: *off A386 north-east of Tavistock*
Open: *12–2.30, 6–11 (Sun 6.30–10.30)*
Bar meals: *lunch and dinner served all week, 12–2, 7–9; average main course £10.95*
Restaurant: *lunch and dinner served all week, 12–2, 7–9*
Brewery/company: *free house*
Principal beers: *Princetown Jail Ale, Interbrew Bass, Summerskills Tamar, Badger Dorset Best*
Children welcome
Dogs allowed
Parking: *40*

A true pub *in the best English tradition and surrounded by moorland on the edge of Dartmoor, this 15th-century inn retains its character with slate floors, low beams and large fireplaces filled with blazing logs in cold weather. In summer the beautiful garden is popular.*

Food is at the centre of the operation, with a regularly changing blackboard menu listing home-made dishes based on fresh local produce. At lunchtime the choice ranges around traditional bar meals and the likes of roast lamb shank, monkfish in creamy garlic sauce, and Devonshire lemon chicken. In the evening the tone is raised a few notches to include caramelised onion tart with brie, and Stilton and pear pâté starters, and main choices such as roast rack of lamb with minted gooseberry sauce, and mushroom, chestnut and leek pie. Known for its real ales, with at least eight wines available by the glass.

5: Climbing up to Golden Cap

The Cap is the highest point on the south coast, at 627 feet (191m), with views along the shore to the tip of Portland Bill in one direction and to Start Point in the other.

Golden Cap is the rather obvious name for a high, flat-topped hill of deep orange sandstone on the cliffs between Charmouth and Bridport. It represents the tail-end of a vein of the warm-coloured sandstone that stretches down from the Cotswolds.

Climbing towards the top, you pass from neat fields, through a line of wind-scoured oak trees, into an area of high heathland, walking up through bracken, heather, bilberry and blackberry, alive with songbirds. The loose undercliff on the seaward side creates a different habitat. In botanical and wildlife terms, Golden Cap is one of the richest properties in the National Trust's portfolio.

On the very top of Golden Cap itself is a simple memorial to the Earl of Antrim, chairman of the National Trust in the 1960s and 1970s. It was he who spearheaded its 1965 appeal campaign, named 'Enterprise Neptune', to purchase sections of unspoiled coastline before the developers moved in and it was all too late. Golden Cap was part of this and over the years the Trust has continued to buy up pockets of land all around, with the aim of preserving the traditional field pattern that exists in the area between Eype and Lyme Regis.

Its acquisition includes the ruined church of St Gabriel's (little more than a low shell with a porch to one side) and the neighbouring row of thatched cottages that have been smartly refurbished and are let out as visitor accommodation. They are all that remains of the fishing village of Stanton, sheltering behind the cliffs, which was largely abandoned after the coast road was rerouted inland in 1824.

The extension walk continues inland to Morcombelake, and finally back over Langdon Hill, also owned by the National Trust. Seen from the speedy A35 coast road, Morcombelake is an unexciting ribbon development, to be hurried through on your way to somewhere else. On foot, however, you discover a network of narrow, winding lanes on the slopes of Langdon Hill that takes you into a different, tranquil world. Rambling houses with old bay windows have a confident, nautical air, as though this was a place for retired admirals.

Walk information

Distance: 4 miles (6.4km) + extension 2½ miles (4km)
Map: OS Explorer 116 Lyme Regis & Bridport
Start/finish: car park (charge) above gravel beach in Seatown (may flood in stormy weather); grid ref SY 420917
Ascent/gradient: 3
Paths: field tracks, country lanes, steep zig-zag gravel path; 7 stiles
Landscape: windswept coastline of lumps and bumps

Looking west to Golden Cap

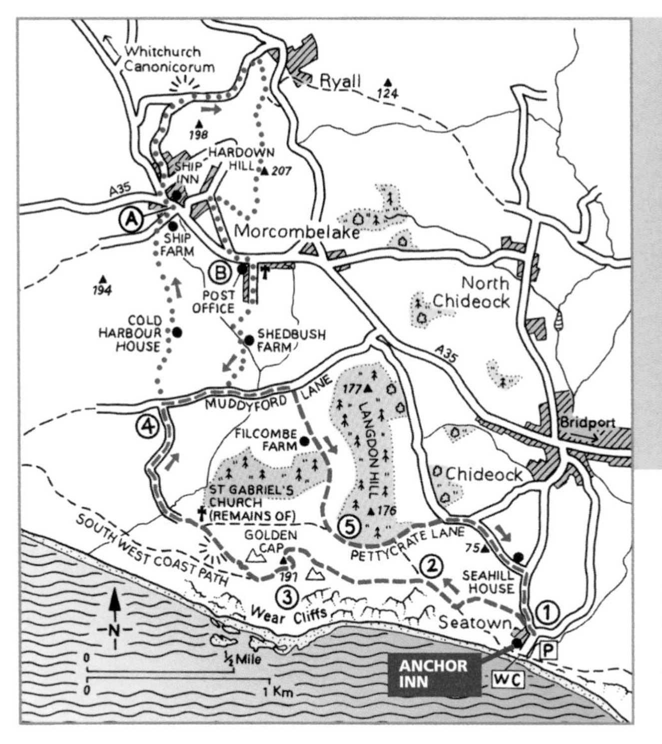

Look for

Moore's biscuit bakery in Morcombelake is a fascinating detour, worth it for the smell alone. Through a glass screen see the biscuits being hand-made – and sample as you watch. There's also a gallery of artwork associated with its packaging. The famous savoury Dorset knobs, thrice-baked and explosively crisp, are a post-Christmas speciality. Open weekdays, and Saturday mornings in summer.

Walk directions

❶ From the car park near the **Anchor Inn**, walk back up through Seatown. Cross a stile on the left, onto the footpath, signposted 'Coast Path Diversion'. Cross a stile at the end, bear left to cross a stile and footbridge into woodland. Cross a pair of stiles at the other side and bear right up the hill, signposted 'Golden Cap'.

❷ Where the track forks keep left. Go through some trees and over a stile. Bear left, straight across the open hillside, with Golden Cap ahead of you. Pass through a line of trees and walk up the fence. Go up some steps, cross a stile and continue ahead. At the fingerpost go left through a gate to follow the path of shallow steps to the top of Golden Cap.

❸ Pass the trig point and turn right along the top. Pass the stone memorial to the Earl of Antrim. At a marker stone turn right and follow the zig-zag path steeply downhill, enjoying views to Charmouth and Lyme Regis. Go through a gate and bear right over the field towards the ruined St Gabriel's Church. In the bottom corner turn down through a gate, passing the ruins on your right, then go through a second gate. Go down the track, passing cottages on the left, and bear right up the road, signed 'Morcombelake'. Follow this up between high banks and hedges which put the wild flowers conveniently at eye-level. Continue through a gateway.

❹ At the road junction, turn right down Muddyford Lane, signed 'Langdon Hill' (or go straight on for the extension). Pass the gate of Shedbush Farm (the extension rejoins) and continue straight up the hill. Turn right up a concreted lane towards Filcombe Farm. Follow blue markers through the farmyard, bearing left through two gates. Walk up the track, go through two more gates and bear left over the top of the green saddle between Langdon Hill and Golden Cap.

❺ Go left through a gate in the corner and down a gravel lane (Pettycrate Lane) beside the woods, signed 'Seatown'. Ignore a footpath off to the right. At a junction of tracks keep right, downhill, with a delectable green patchwork of fields on the hillside ahead. Pass Seahill House on the left and turn right, onto a road. Continue down this into Seatown village to return to the inn.

Anchor Inn

Seatown, Chideock DT6 6JU
Tel: 01297 489215
Directions: *at Chideock turn south off the A35, opposite the church, and follow the single track road down to the beach.*
Open: *11–2.30, 6–11 (summer 11–11)*
Bar meals: *lunch and dinner served all week, 12–2, 6.30–9.30*
Brewery/company: *Palmers*
Principal beers: *Palmers 200 Premium Ale, IPA, Copper Ale*
Children welcome
Dogs allowed
Parking: *20*

The Anchor Inn *is blessed with its setting smack on the Dorset coastal path, and makes the most of its position with a large sun terrace and cliffside beer garden overlooking the beach. On winter weekdays it is blissfully quiet, while the summer sees it thronging with holidaymakers. The rusted anchor outside belonged to the* Hope, *wrecked on Chesil Beach during a storm in January 1748. The crew escaped to safety, but the ship broke up, shedding £50,000 worth of gold, silver and other valuables, creating a mini gold-rush.*

The menu here offers something for everyone, and what is not shown there is likely to be found on the special blackboard. Plenty of seafood, including crab and lobster, and game in season. Typical dishes are monkfish in Thai sauce, game casserole, carbonade of beef, and vegetable and spinach pancakes, plus sandwiches, burgers and jacket potatoes.

Extension to Morcombelake

For a longer walk, at Point ❹ on the main walk go straight ahead, onto the broad track and follow it up the valley, with Chardown and Stonebarrow hills up to the left. A former radar station on Stonebarrow Hill now accommodates the National Trust's volunteer working parties. There is also an information point and shop during summer (access by road from Charmouth). Pass Cold Harbour House on the right. Go through two gates. At a road bear right and keep right, past Ship Farm to the A35, Point Ⓐ.

Cross with care and turn left at the Ship Inn. Take the first road right up the hill, signposted 'Whitchurch Canonicorum'. Almost immediately turn right and bear left up Pitmans Lane. This narrow road wraps itself around the hilltop, offering glimpses into the nooks and crannies of Morcombelake. There are extensive views down to the left to Whitchurch Canonicorum, dominated by its church. Look left by Pitmans House for a clear view down to Charmouth.

Carry straight on as Taylors Lane feeds in from the left, leaving the houses behind for the wilder tops. At a gate bear right, up a footpath by a fingerpost, towards the heath. After rising, this leads round the back of the hill into a quiet green world with lovely views over the valley. Look for the crossing of a deep-cut path – turn right, up this. Bear right at the top, up the track. Turn left by the National Trust sign and follow this broad track, up over the top of the exposed heath on Hardown Hill.

Pass a bench on the left, then follow the track round and down, to emerge at a road junction. Turn left and walk down Gibbs Lane to meet the A35 near the post office, Point Ⓑ.

Cross and turn left. Moore's biscuit shop (see page 20)is just ahead, but turn off to the right before it, down Shedbush Lane. At the bottom cross a stile and bear right along the field edge. Continue down to a gate and bear left through Shedbush Farm, a splendid brick and thatch affair. Follow the farm drive down to the road and turn left, rejoining the main walk on Muddyford Lane.

Walk information

Distance: 4½ miles (7.2km)
Map: OS Explorer 117 Cerne Abbas & Bere Regis
Start/finish: Acorn Inn; grid ref SY 572045
Ascent/gradient: 2
Paths: tracks, paths and estate roads
Landscape: farmland and parkland

A shady copse of oak trees

6: Discovering Hardy Country in Dorset

A gentle walk from Evershot to Melbury Osmond.

The walks starts at a pub which featured in Thomas Hardy's *Tess of the D'Urbervilles*.

Walk directions

❶ From the historic **Acorn Inn** head left down Fore Street to the village green. Bear left here and make your way along the tarmac road through the Melbury estate. Keep dogs on a lead along here.

❷ Take the first right turning and follow the gravel track uphill and down the far side, passing a conifer woodland. Keep left where another route branches off to the right and pass a pond on the left.

❸ Further on, look for a large private lake on the right. Turn right just beyond it to a gate, cross a bridge and go through a second gate. Head straight across the field, keeping the fence on your right. Look for a small concealed gate in the far right-hand corner, leading into an oak copse. Once through the gate, veer left along the track and down to a cottage by the road.

❹ Follow the tree-lined track to the right of the property and enter a field when it terminates at a gate. Make for a small waymarked gate over to the right and follow the often wet and muddy path beside a stream to a bridge. Cross it and pass under a stone bridge, bearing left. Pass several thatched cottages before reaching the road.

❺ Bear left and keep on the road as it runs through the Melbury estate and back to Evershot. Dogs should be on a lead again along this stretch. Begin a gentle climb, and soon the outline of Melbury House looms into view. Pass right round the house and through the deer park on the other side. Now the road climbs quite steeply before descending to Evershot village green.

❻ To avoid the main street, turn right along Back Lane to a left-hand footpath which leads back to the pub car park.

Acorn Inn

Evershot DT2 0JW
Tel: 01935 83228
Directions: *A303 to Yeovil, then the Dorchester road; turn right off A37 to Evershot*
Open: *11.30–3, 6–11*
Bar meals: *lunch and dinner served all week, 12–2, 6.30–9*
Restaurant: *lunch and dinner served all week, 12–2, 7–9*
Brewery/company: *free house*
Principal beers: *Fuller's London Pride, Butcombe, Palmer*
Children welcome
Dogs allowed
Parking: *30*
Rooms: *9 bedrooms en suite from s£60, d£80*

A fine stone *building, the Acorn Inn has been carefully restored to create the perfect rural base from which to explore Hardy Country and the beautiful Dorset coastline. Thomas Hardy wrote about this 16th-century inn as 'the Sow and Acorn' in* Tess of the D'Urbervilles, *and is believed to have stayed here when writing* Jude the Obscure. *The pub still has a sleepy village setting, surrounded by fabulous countryside and some great walks. The dining room used to be a grand hall, thought to have been used by Judge Jeffreys as a courthouse, and the old stables have been converted into a skittle alley. There are two oak-panelled bars with flagstone floors, and log fires in carved Hamstone fireplaces. The bars serve traditional ales and a selection of wines.*

In addition to the choice of bar food, such as hearty soups and substantial sandwiches, a full menu is offered in the Hardy Dining Room or the no-smoking restaurant. Fresh fish from nearby Bridport and local game are specialities which frequently feature on the short menu. Fish options may range from cod in beer batter with mushy peas, to grilled red snapper on crushed potato with pesto. Other options include local estate game casserole with port and juniper berries, or loin of pork with wild mushroom sauce. A tempting array of puddings takes in a traditional apple crumble, and a white chocolate parfait with dark chocolate sauce.

Accommodation is provided in individually styled rooms, with two four-poster beds.

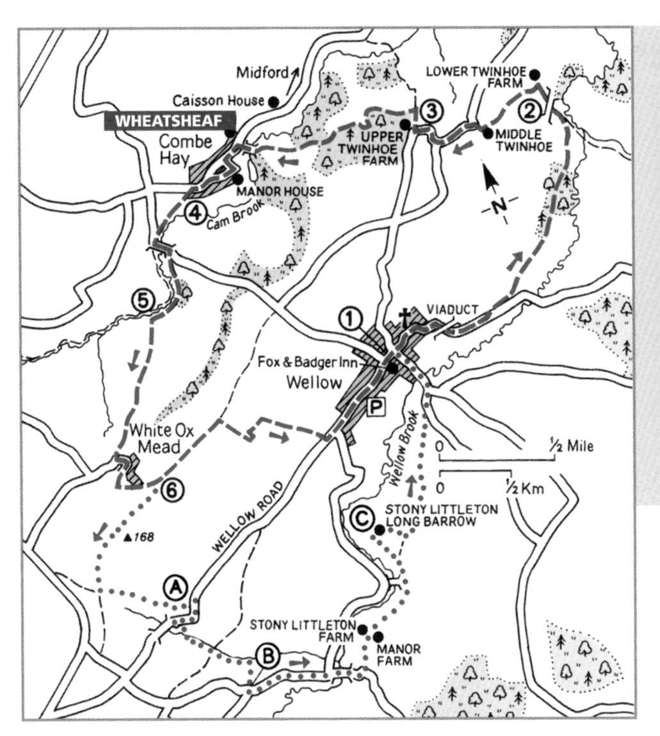

Walk information

Distance: 6½ miles (10.4km) + extension 2½ miles (4km)
Map: OS Explorer 142 Shepton Mallet
Start/finish: street parking in village centre, or car park below Peasedown Rd; grid ref ST 739583
Ascent/gradient: 2
Paths: byways, stream sides and some field paths; 12 stiles
Landscape: grassy hillsides and valleys
Note: a torch is useful to explore the long barrow

7: Where the Cotswolds meet the Mendips

When you walk through this quiet corner of Somerset, it certainly doesn't strike you as an industrial landscape.

You may, for example, wonder why such a sleepy valley ever needed its own railway. As you climb out of the Wellow Valley you might notice some odd conical hills. And then, at Combe Hay, with its lovely medieval manor house, there is some very peculiar 18th-century brickwork. Combe Hay and Wellow were actually at the heart of Somerset's industrial revolution. And the last coal mine here only closed in the 1970s.

Like so much in Somerset, it started with the Romans. In the Temple of Minerva in nearby Bath, a fire burned – according to some historians, a living coal fire. Certainly by the 16th century the mines were going down.

Squashed between the Mendips and the Cotswolds, the Somerset coal field is small and awkward. Many of the veins are vertical, and only a few feet (a metre or so) in width. So coal might be hacked from overhead, on an improvised platform jammed across a narrow shaft. And always, for miner and mine owner alike, there was the threat of cheaper and easier coal coming up the River Avon from Wales.

This brings us to the engineering bricks in the field at Combe Hay. To move 100,000 tons of coal a year to Bath, a canal was constructed that was ambitious even by the standards of the enterprising 18th century. Over its length of just 10 miles (16km), from Paulton Basin to Bath, the Somersetshire Coal Canal had two aqueducts and a tunnel.

Furthermore, there was the problem of the 165-foot (50-m) climb on to Combe Hay Hill. The solution was, in effect, an underwater elevator. A barge on the upper canal entered a floating

Look for

In all but the driest of conditions, the ascent towards White Ox Mead features some of the stickiest mud anywhere. The reason is fuller's earth: this is the special sort of clay (aluminium silicate) that was mined and used to wash wool with – as well as grease, it also absorbs water. The consequent swelling is what caused the caisson shaft at Combe Hay to bulge inwards and jam.

While there

Radstock Museum gives much of its space to the coal industry. It has a reconstructed mine tunnel and items from that most attractive of ages (to look at afterwards if not to live through), the industrial 18th century.

metal box called a caisson. The caisson was sealed, and water pumped in until it started to sink. It sank for 50 feet (15m) to the bottom of the shaft. Its door was then matched up to a door in the base of the shaft; both doors were opened; and the barge floated out. The process would take seven minutes, unless the caisson got stuck. The ground around the caisson shaft is fuller's earth, which expands when wetted, and this may have caused the sides of the shaft to bulge inwards. The caissons were abandoned after only two years and replaced with an inclined plane.

The southern branch of the canal, through Wellow to Radstock, was never completed. Instead, a horse-drawn tramway carried the coal out. Both canal and tramway were replaced by the railway, which in its turn has been superseded by motor roads.

Walk directions

❶ Head out past the church and under a viaduct. Immediately after Wellow Trekking a track starts just above the road. Where it becomes unclear, cross to the hedge opposite and continue above it. A new track runs through a wood, then down to the valley floor. Where a bridleway sign points right, turn left to pass under a railway bridge.

❷ Just before Lower Twinhoe Farm turn left into a signposted green track. At the hilltop the track fades into thistly ground. Bear right, before Middle Twinhoe, to a small gate. Turn right along the farm's driveway to a lane. Turn left, then to the right around farm buildings and bend left towards Upper Twinhoe. Just before this farm a signed track descends to the right.

❸ After 130 yards (118m) turn left through a double gate and along a field top. The path then slants down through scrubby woodland towards Combe Hay. From the wood edge follow the lower edge of a field to a stone bridge into the village, with the **Wheatsheaf** pub ahead to your right. Follow the main road left, to pass the Manor House.

❹ After the last house of Combe Hay, find a gap in the wall on the left. Bear right, down to the Cam Brook, and follow it to a road bridge. Cross it and continue with the stream down on your right through a field and a wood. Follow the stream along another field to a stile, then along the foot of a short field to a gateway.

❺ Don't go through this gateway, but turn up the field edge to a stile on the right instead. Slant up left across the next field to a nettly way between high thorns. At the top of this bear right in a rutted track to a lane. Turn uphill to White Ox Mead, and follow the lane for another 60 yards (55m) to a stile. Slant up to another stile, and turn up a tarred track to where it divides near a shed without walls.

❻ Keep ahead on a rutted track along the hill crest. Ignore a waymarked stile to pass under low- and high-voltage electric cables. Here a small metal gate on the right leads to a hoof-printed path down beside a fence. At the foot of the field turn left, then left again (uphill), round a corner to a gate. Turn left across the field top and down its edge to the street leading into Wellow.

Extension to Stony Littleton

For a longer walk, at Point ❻ of the main route turn right above the shed without walls. The track becomes a narrow way between overgrown banks as it descends into the valley of the Wellow Brook. Where it reaches a gate, turn left into a hedged path that becomes a wide, muddy track to reach Wellow Road, Point Ⓐ.

Turn right along the lane as it dips to a bridge. Here turn left through two grey gates into a tractor graveyard. Bear right to cross the stream, and head down alongside it over four stiles. Cross a stony, sunken track to another stile; continue downstream, through two more fields, until a track leads up to the right to join a lane, Point **B**.

Turn left, downhill, to cross a bridge over the Wellow Brook. After 130 yards (118m) turn left into a track, signposted 'Manor Farm'. This passes below the fine manor house and above Stony Littleton Farm into a grassy track. Slant down left to join the stream beside a long footbridge. Do not cross this bridge, but take a stile ahead with an English Heritage waymarker. Go up with a hedge on your left to join a green track, but before the top of this turn left over a stile. Follow the field top until a signposted stile leads up to Stony Littleton Long Barrow (Point **C**).

Built in the New Stone Age (about 5,000 years ago), the long barrow has a low, stone entrance at its southern end, leading to a passage with grave chambers on either side. A fossil ammonite is displayed at the entrance. The roof has been recently repaired by English Heritage – the damage was started by a farmer in 1760 seeking stone for track repairs. The interior should now be safe; but even so it would be wise to leave one member of the party outside in case of accident.

From the barrow entrance head uphill to a hedge gap, and turn left alongside this hedge. Contour across the following field to a gate with track beyond. Where this reaches a lane, turn down left. The road crosses a ford, with a stone footbridge alongside, then rises into Wellow village.

Wheatsheaf

Combe Hay BA2 7EG
Tel: 01225 833504
Directions: *take A369 Exeter road from Bath to Odd Down, turn left at park towards Combe Hay; follow lane for 2 miles (3.2km) to a thatched cottage and turn left*
Open: *11–2.30, 6–10.30 (Sun 12–3, 7–10.30)*
Bar meals: *lunch and dinner served all week, 12–2, 6.30–9.30*
Restaurant: *lunch and dinner served all week, 12–2, 6.30–9.30*
Brewery/company: *free house*
Principal beers: *Courage Best, John Smith, Old Speckled Hen*
Children welcome
Dogs allowed
Parking: *100*
Rooms: *3 bedrooms en suite from s£55, d£80*

Nestling on a *hillside overlooking a peaceful valley, 2 miles (3.2km) south of Bath off the A367, the 17th-century Wheatsheaf is a pretty black-and-white timbered pub. It's adorned with flowers in summer, and has an attractive landscaped terrace garden – the ideal spot for summer imbibing. Peter Wilkins took over in November 2000 and has maintained the unspoilt character of the rambling bar, complete with massive solid wooden tables, sporting prints and open log fire.*

Food on the varied carte features home-cooked dishes, notably local game in season and fresh fish. Typical choices may include ploughman's lunches, terrines, and locally caught trout, in addition to roast rack of lamb, breast of pheasant stuffed with cream cheese, mushrooms and garlic, and chicken filled with crab and prawns and wrapped in bacon.

Comfortable overnight accommodation is in a converted stable block.

8: A country wander from Wells

Enjoy a rural diversion in the famous cathedral city.

Walk information

Distance: 6 miles (9.7km)
Map: OS Explorer 141 Cheddar Gorge & Mendip Hills West
Start/finish: Fountain Inn; grid ref ST 551459
Gradient: 2
Paths: roads, paths; 3 stiles
Landscape: rolling hills and wooded combes

The 12th-century cathedral of Wells

Walk directions

❶ From the **Fountain Inn** turn into Vicar's Close and make for a narrow alleyway and some steps at the top. Turn right at the road and then left into College Road. Follow it to the A39.

❷ Turn right and swing left into Walcombe Lane, passing Walcombe Farmhouse. Keep right at the fork and turn right at the next junction. Take the bridleway on the right, further up the hill. Follow the sunken woodland path and turn sharp right at a junction, following the path along the grassy slopes and round to the right by a footpath sign. Keep to the hedgerow, right, and head for a junction of tracks further down.

❸ Turn left, pass Pen Hill Farm and continue ahead on the tarmac track. Pass a house called College and reach a T-junction.

❹ Turn left and walk along to the A39. Cross over by a cottage, turn right and follow the path down the field boundary to a gate. Keep ahead along the woodland edge with a stream on the right. Cross a footbridge and follow the path just outside the trees. Re-enter the woodland and ascend the grassy slope to a seat.

5 Turn right here and keep a house on the left. Follow the grassy path to a stile. Cross the field, keeping to the left perimeter. Avoid the first stile and cross the second. Turn right and skirt the field to a kissing gate. Follow steps down through trees to a stream and cross a stone bridge.

6 Go over the junction and uphill, signposted Hawkers Lane. On reaching the field edge, keep left to a stile and cut through trees and alongside a fence. Pass through a kissing gate and continue ahead in the field. Pass a gate, right, and follow the path as it curves left in line with the boundary. Walk down towards some houses and reach the road. Turn left and cut through the housing estate to the B3139. Turn right here and return to the inn.

Fountain Inn

1 St Thomas Street, Wells BA5 2UU
Tel: 01749 672317
Directions: *from city centre, follow signs to Harringtons; at junction of Tor Street and St Thomas Street*
Open: *10.30–2.30, 6–11 (Sun 12–3, 7–10.30)*
Bar meals: *lunch and dinner served all week, 12–2.30, 6–10; average main course £6.50*
Restaurant: *lunch and dinner served all week, 12–2.30, from 6; average 3 course £18.50*
Brewery/company: *Innspired*
Principal beers: *Butcombe Bitter, Interbrew Bass, Scottish Courage, Courage Best*
Children welcome
Parking: *24*

Situated barely a *stone's throw from Wells Cathedral, this 16th-century inn takes its name from the spring that feeds the conduit in the city. It is reputed to have housed the labourers who helped to build the cathedral, but since the great church was completed by 1465, the tale is probably apocryphal. In no doubt at all, though, is its reputation for good quality food and wines. This side of the business has been built up by the present owners, who fell in love with the place when they visited Wells 20 years ago. The Fountain is just around the corner from Vicar's Close, a row of medieval houses built specially for the Vicar's Choral, and it has long been a favourite haunt of the cathedral choir.*

Nowadays its popularity has spread much further afield, fuelled in part by the locally brewed Butcombe Bitter and other decent ales, which are served in the unpretentious ground-floor bar. The bar menu includes extensive choices for brunch, and also features roasts, specials, and cream teas. In Boxer's upstairs restaurant choices include starters like chilled melon with raspberry coulis, and smoked salmon roses with a lemon vinaigrette. Main course options such as fruity chicken curry, beef, ale and mushroom pie, and speciality sausages with seasoned mash and red wine gravy. Finish with rum and raisin torte, or treacle sponge and custard.

9: Heytesbury and the Wylye Valley

The Wylye, one of Wiltshire's lesser-known chalk streams, threads its way through some of the finest downland scenery on its 22-mile (35-km) journey from Warminster to Salisbury.

Iron-Age hill forts and ancient tumuli and barrows litter the rolling chalk downland, much of it now extensively farmed. In the valley slumber pretty picture-postcard villages, including the charmingly named Knook, Boyton, Sherrington and Corton, which are visited on the extension walk.

Lying just 3 miles (4.8km) east of Warminster, Heytesbury is an ancient borough with a rich history. Wealth and prosperity came to the village through the prominence of one influential family in the 14th century – the Hungerfords – who acquired land and purchased manors across the south-west, including a complex of manors in the upper Wylye Valley. Sir Walter Hungerford fought at Agincourt in 1415 and became Treasurer of England in 1428. He also founded and endowed a chapel in Salisbury Cathedral and founded the Almshouses, or Hospital of St John, that stand opposite the homely **Angel Inn**. Under the Hungerfords, the Wylye estates became noted for sheep farming and Heytesbury village became the main wool warehouse of the family.

Cloth production began here in the mid-15th century, but it was not until the 18th century that the proximity of the River Wylye attracted cloth mills along its course. Plans to develop the industry to match that of nearby Warminster never materialised, and when its borough status was lost in 1832 Heytesbury gradually declined.

In 1926 Heytesbury House became the home of the World War I poet and writer Siegfried Sassoon. He grew to love the dramatic views and wide horizons of Wiltshire's downland when he was stationed in the area during training on Salisbury Plain. This inspired him to buy Heytesbury Manor. Following his death in 1967, it was occupied by his son George until 1994.

Walk directions

❶ Head east along the village street, pass the **Angel Inn** and turn right down Mantles Lane. Where it curves right to become Mill Lane, take the footpath left along a drive beside the River Wylye. Bear right on to the footpath in front of Mantles Cottage, go through a walk-through stile and walk along the right-hand edge of pasture, soon to bear slightly left on nearing Mill Farm to reach a gate.

❷ Beyond a further gate, turn right across the bridge, then follow the yellow arrow left and soon cross a footbridge. Follow the Wessex Ridgeway marker straight ahead at a junction of ways then, just before a further footbridge, turn left through a gap and bear right along the field edge. At a white wooden arrow, bear half left across the field towards thatched

Walk information

Distance: 4 miles (6.4km) + extension 4½ miles (7.2km)
Map: OS Explorer 143 Warminster & Trowbridge
Start/finish: along wide village street; grid ref ST 926425
Ascent/gradient: 1
Paths: field paths and bridleways; 10 stiles
Landscape: river valley and lofty chalk downland

Look for

In Knook, note the interesting stone tympanum above the south door of St Margaret's Church. The intricate carved motifs are early 11th century. Boyton church is the resting place of the chivalrous crusader Sir Alexander Gifford, whose striking effigy shows him cross-legged with an otter at his feet.

While there

Seek out the hamlet of Tytherington across the valley from Heytesbury to view the single-cell chapel that dates from 1083. It was endowed by Empress Matilda, mother of Henry II, in 1140. At Codford St Mary you will find the second largest Anzac War Grave Cemetery in Britain, with the graves of nearly 100 New Zealand and Australian troops who died on the battlefields during World War I.

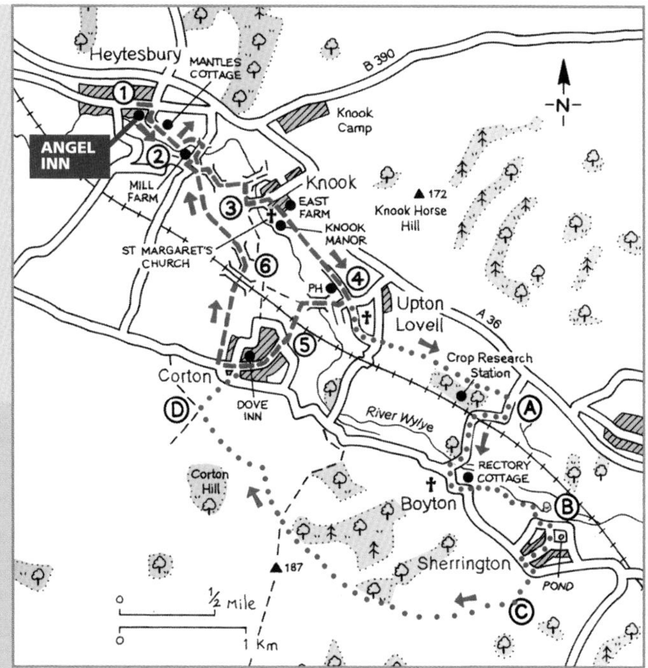

cottages to the river bank, and bear right to a stile and junction of paths.

❸ Turn left across the footbridge, pass Knook Manor and St Margaret's Church, then turn right by the post-box and soon pass East Farm on a track. At two gates, go through the left-hand gate and proceed ahead along the right-hand field edge to another gate. Continue on into Upton Lovell.

❹ At a crossroads, take the signed footpath right, then just before the drive to Hatch House, follow the path left to a footbridge over the river. Go through a gate and proceed ahead along the field edge to a metal gate. Cross the stile on your left, walk along the hedged path and cross the railway with great care via gates and steps. Continue to a lane in Corton.

❺ Turn left through the village, eventually passing the Dove Inn. At the T-junction, take the arrowed path across the stile on your right. Head across the field on a defined path to a stile. Keep ahead along the fenced path to a further stile and proceed along the right-hand edge of the field. Shortly, climb a stile and turn left along the field edge to a stile and soon pass beneath the railway.

❻ Cross a footbridge and then a stile and walk beside the right-hand fence to a gate. From here, follow the grassy track ahead. Cross another stile and keep to the track until you reach a lane.

Turn right and follow it through the complex of buildings at Mill Farm and across the river to rejoin your outward route beside the River Wylye back into Heytesbury.

Extension to Sherrington

At the crossroads, Point ❹, keep straight on to the church and then follow the path ahead to a drive. Turn left, then left again at the lane, soon to bear off right at the bend onto a bridleway. Enter a field and keep right along the edge to the corner. Keep ahead along a straight path through a tunnel of trees to a field. Proceed straight across towards a bungalow, crossing two stiles to a lane, Point Ⓐ. Turn right and continue across the railway and the River Wylye into Boynton, with the handsome St Mary's Church.

At the junction turn right, then left in 150 yards (137m) to visit Boynton Church. Otherwise turn left, pass Rectory Cottage then, at a right-hand bend, cross the stile ahead and turn left around the edge of two fields to a stile. Continue to a gate and turn right on a drive. Bear left into Sherrington, Point Ⓑ, with its intriguing old church.

Turn right through the village, passing the pond, and turn left at the T-junction. In 100 yards (91m), cross the stile on the right and walk up the left-hand field edge to a stile. Turn right and soon bear diagonally left uphill to a stile. Continue to a further stile and turn right along the track, Point Ⓒ. Look back across the valley to view the Rising Sun Badge etched into Lamb Down in 1916 by Australian troops stationed in the area.

Angel Inn

High Street, Heytsbury BA12 0ED
Tel: 01985 840330
Directions: *From A303 take A36 toward Bath, and after 8 miles (12.8km) Heytsbury is on the left*
Open: *11.30–3, 6.30–11 (Sun 12–10.30)*
Bar meals: *lunch and dinner served all week, 12–2.30, 7–9.30; average main course £9.95*
Restaurant: *lunch and dinner served all week, 12–2.30, 7–9.30; average 3 course à la carte £20*
Brewery/company: *free house*
Principal beers: *Ringwood Best, Marstons Pedigree, Old Hosky, Ringwood Boondoogle*
Children welcome
Dogs allowed
Parking: *12*
Rooms: *8 bedrooms en suite from s£50, d£65*

A dining pub *in the modern idiom, the Angel preserves all the charm and character of a traditional coaching inn. You'll find it tucked away in a tiny village in the lovely Wyley Valley, on the edge of Salisbury Plain, just a few minutes' drive from Warminster. It's well placed for exploring Bath, Salisbury and the nearby Longleat Estate.*

There's a reassuringly civilised atmosphere within, the long beamed bar featuring scrubbed pine tables, warmly decorated walls and a fireplace with a wood-burning stove. A separate lounge area with squashy sofas and easy chairs leads through to the neat rear dining room. In summer, guests spill out into the secluded courtyard garden, which is furnished with hardwood tables and cotton parasols. Relaxed and friendly service makes for a pleasurable dining experience.

Comprehensive seasonal menus are based on good quality produce approached with flair and imagination. Lighter/starter dishes include glazed goats' cheese on a toasted croûton and salad leaves, and baked stuffed field mushroom. For something more substantial try Wylye Valley trout with sautéed new potatoes and fennel salad, rack of lamb with pimento peppers, sautéed garlic potatoes and thyme jus, or perhaps panfried guinea fowl with crisp potato rösti, wilted pousse and cherry tomatoes.Round off your meal with cappuchino crème brûleé. pineapple sorbet, or chocolate and orange pudding, and enjoy a coffee by the open fire.

Gradually ascend, keep right on merging with a farm road and continue for 1¾ miles (2.8km) to reach a crossing of routes, Point Ⓓ. Turn right, then almost immediately bear left down a bridleway into Corton. Cross the lane and descend to the lane opposite the Dove Inn. Turn left and join the main walk just after Point ❺.

10: Roaming the woods of Ashley Hill

This pretty walk crosses the parkland of Hall Place, now the Berkshire College of Agriculture, before reaching the delightful tree-clad slopes of Ashley Hill.

While there

Visit the Shire Horse Centre at Maidenhead Thicket, 2 mile (3.2km) west of Maidenhead. You can meet the gentle giants, enjoy a dray ride, explore the saddler's workshop and the harness display, and take a welcome break in the tearoom. Open from March to October.

Walk information

Distance: 4 miles (6.4km)
Map: Explorer 172 Chiltern Hills East, High Wycombe, Maidenhead
Start/finish: Crown, Burchetts Green; grid ref SU 840813
Ascent/gradient: 2
Paths: roads, field paths, woodland tracks; several stiles
Landscape: parkland and woodland

A shire horse at the Shire Horse Centre

Walk directions

1 From the **Crown** pub cross over at the junction into Hall Place Lane. When you reach the entrance to Lane End House, follow the footpath to the left of it. Make for a kissing gate and then take the path across the field towards an avenue of limes.

2 Swing left at the avenue, and then bear right as the drive forks in front of Hall Place. Pass the veterinary surgery before veering half-left at the waymark. After the barns and animal enclosures, follow the track down between the trees and bushes to a crossroads. Keep left at the fork just beyond it and take the clear track towards High Wood.

3 Make for a gate and cut through the wood to the far side, where there are impressive views across the Thames Valley. Swing left and walk along the woodland edge to two gates and a waymark. Bear left here, cutting back through the woods to a gate.

4 Head south across the fields, cross two farm tracks and go through a kissing gate into a field. Take the gate in the far boundary and follow the path through light woodland and up steps to the next gate. Continue ahead in the next field, passing a house with a conservatory before reaching a stile. Turn right down the lane.

5 Keep ahead when it bends right and pass the turning to the Dewdrop Inn. Follow the path ahead at the 'no through road' sign, turn left at a waymarked junction, cross a track and veer left at the fork. Swing left at the house ahead in the trees and follow the drive down through the wood. As it bends right, go forward on a path to the road.

6 Keep right and walk along a path on the left. Cross two stiles and follow a fence and stream to a track by an oak tree. Go straight on to two stiles by the houses of Burchetts Green. Turn left at the road and return to the **Crown.**

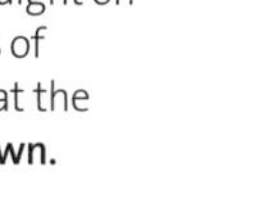

Crown

Burchetts Green, nr Maidenhead
SL6 6QZ
Tel: 01628 822844
Directions: *from the M4 take the A404(M), then 3rd exit*
Open: *12–3, 6–11*
Bar meals: *lunch and dinner served all week, 12–2.30, 6.30–10; average main course £10*
Restaurant: *lunch and dinner served all week, 12–2.30, 7–10; average 3 course à la carte £25*
Brewery/company: *Greene King*
Principal beers: *Greene King IPA, Ruddles Best, Wadworth 6X*
Children welcome
Parking: *30*

In the middle *of a small hamlet and overlooking the village green, this local stands amid a large rose garden, bedecked with handsome garden furniture. Nearby Ashley Hill woods are a haven for naturalists and walkers, who often stop by for a pint of real ale. Inside, the whitewashed walls and low, beamed ceilings create a welcoming atmosphere, particularly in the intimate dining room, where the tables are decorated with vases of fresh flowers.*

Do not expect to pop in for a quick snack, as everything is cooked to order from the freshest available ingredients. Tempting main dishes on a short, daily menu may be large grilled Dover Sole, calves' liver with bacon and creamed potatoes, monkfish, roast duck with black cherry and brandy sauce, or perhaps warm chicken salad with bacon and avocado. Reservations are advised from Friday to Sunday to be sure of a table.

11: A woodland walk from a classic country pub

Our pubs are unique to this country but how exactly did they begin? The story of the English pub spans more than 1,000 years of history, beginning with the dismal alehouses of the Anglo-Saxon period.

Walk information

Distance: 3½ miles (5.7km)
Map: OS Explorer 158 Newbury & Hungerford
Start/finish: space at side of Pot Kiln, Frilsham; grid ref SU 551731
Ascent/gradient: 2
Paths: tracks, paths and stretches of country road
Landscape: woodland on northern side of Pang Valley

Later came the old drovers' hostelries, followed by coaching inns and then Georgian and Victorian pubs built to take advantage of the canal and railway trade. Finally, today, we have the familiar theme boozer which bears little resemblance to the traditional image of the genuine, authentic local.

The **Pot Kiln** is a famous tavern in an isolated part of Berkshire. The pub is located down a narrow country lane, hidden among trees, and is quite hard to find. In fact, there is not another house in sight. There have been many additions and various changes to the inn over the years, but, thankfully, the Pot Kiln still retains its original character. Many of its supporters feel it should have a protection order slapped on it, so that it can be preserved for all time as a permanent reminder of how country pubs used to be.

From the outside, the inn could almost pass for a farm or a private house. Inside, there are two bars – lounge and public – and between them is an off-sales hatch in the panelled lobby. In 2001 the landlords celebrated 20 years at the Pot Kiln – an excellent testimony to their success.

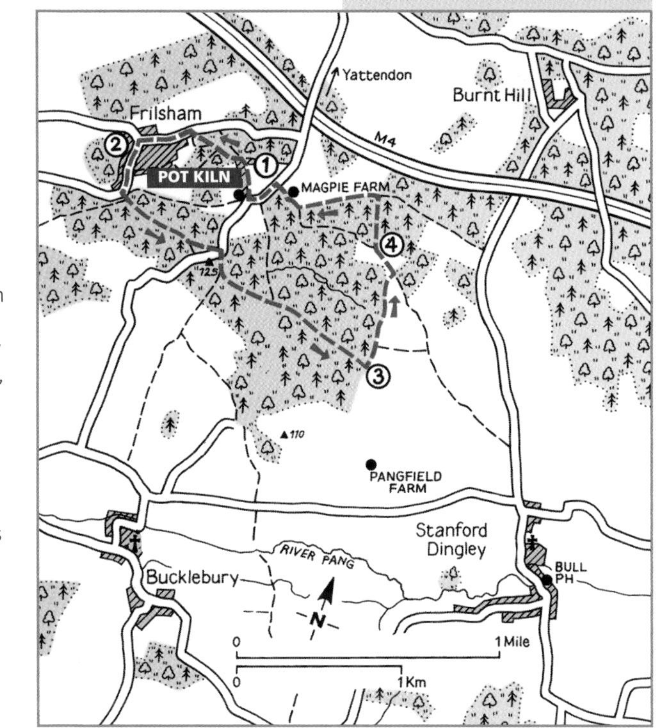

Walk directions

1 Go to the end of the car park at the side of the **Pot Kiln** and follow the track. Keep the microbrewery on your left and pass several houses, including Laurel Bank Cottages. Avoid a public footpath on the left and continue to two cottages at right angles to the byway. Bear left just beyond them and follow a footpath between holly trees. Disregard the turning on the left and keep right at the next fork. Head for the road and turn left. Walk through Frilsham village, pass Beechfield, a

residential development, and turn left at the sign for Hermitage and Bucklebury.

❷ When the lane bends right, go straight ahead, following the path deep into the woods. Pass through a gate and continue on the bridleway to the next waymark. Branch off to the left at this point, following the path down the wooded slope to the road. Cross over to a gateway and continue ahead on the track. Piles of logs can often be seen lining the route here, waiting to be transported to the sawmills. Pass a waymarked track on the right and continue on the main track, following it through ornamental woodland to the next waymarked junction.

❸ Bear left here and cut through bluebell woods to a gate. Cross the field to a gate in the next boundary, with traffic on the M4 visible in the distance. Veer half-left in the field and away to the right in the distance, you can just make out the façade of Yattendon Court, up among the trees. Cross the field and make for a bridleway on the right, running into the trees.

❹ Beyond the wood, follow the path between fences and swing left at the next waymarked junction. Walk along to the next junction, where there are footpath and bridleway signs, and veer right. Follow the track round the side of Magpie Farm and on reaching the road, turn left. Return to the car park by the **Pot Kiln.**

Look for

The Yattendon Estate supplies Christmas trees to places from Land's End to John o'Groats, and with more than 1.8 million trees planted over 600 acres (243ha), it is one of Britain's biggest producers. Around 150,000 Christmas trees are sold here every year. Walking through the estate reveals the sheer scale and size of the operation.

Pot Kiln

Frilsham RG18 0XX
Tel: 01635 201366
Directions: *from the A34 towards Oxford, turn first left to Chieveley, then first right to Hermitage; take the second left onto the B4009, second right to Yattendon, right on a sharp left bend, and on for 1 mile (1.6km)*
Open: *11–3, 6.30–11 (Sun 12–3, 7–10.30)*
Bar meals: *lunch and dinner served Wed–Mon, 12–2, 7–9.30; average main course £7.50*
Brewery/company: *free house*
Principal beers: *West Berkshire Brick Kiln, Morlands Original, Arkell's 3B, West Berkshire Resolution*
Dogs allowed
Parking: *30*
Note: *no credit cards*

With relaxing views *across open fields to woodland from its peaceful garden, this timeless 400-year-old brick pub is justifiably popular among walkers, cyclists and real ale enthusiasts. It takes its name from being on the site of old brick kilns, which were her until the beginning of World War II. Outbuildings now house the West Berkshire brewery, set up in 1995. They brew the Brick Kiln Bitter exclusively for the pub. There's a delightfully old-fashioned interior with lobby bar, simple wooden furnishings and warming open fires. It's all spotlessly kept.*

In keeping, the food here is simple and hearty, including filled rolls, salmon fishcakes with fresh vegetables, lamb rogan josh, and steak and kidney pudding.

12: On location at Turville village

A visit to the charming Chiltern village of Turville leaves you with the impression that you may have been here before.

In fact, it's more than likely you have been to Turville without ever leaving the comfort of your armchair. Puzzled? Then look a little closer as you begin this walk and you'll find the answer is quite simple.

Turville is one of Britain's most frequently used film and television locations. Its picturesque cottages and secluded setting at the bottom of a remote valley make it an obvious choice for movie makers and production companies. Over the years the village has featured regularly both on the large and small screen. Two notable productions in recent years have brought Turville to the attention of a new generation of television audiences. The BBC comedy *The Vicar of Dibley*, starring Dawn French, is filmed in the village and the tiny cottage by the entrance to the church doubles as the vicar's home.

And in 1998 the village was extensively used in the award-winning ITV drama *Goodnight Mister Tom*, with the late John Thaw. This quirky wartime story was an immediate hit, and Turville's classic village 'Englishness' was the programme's cornerstone.

One of Britain's most famous wartime propaganda movies was filmed at Turville. *Went the Day Well*, based on a short story by Grahame Greene, dates back to 1942 and illustrates how a small English village is captured by German fifth columnists. Several locals and ex-residents of Turville recall how they moved props on a handcart and pushed rolls of barbed wire on cartwheels, which were used in the film as blockades. The Old School House, by the green, was the local police station in the story.

Overlooking the village is Cobstone Mill, an 18th-century smock mill, which has also played a key part in various productions. The windmill was used in a 1976 episode of *The New Avengers* television series, and also appeared in the children's film classic *Chitty Chitty Bang Bang* (1968). It starred Dick Van Dyke as eccentric Caractacus Potts, who transforms an old racing car into a wondrous flying toy. The family in the story (originally written by James Bond creator Ian Flemming) lived in the windmill.

Walk information

Distance: 3 miles (4.8km) + extension 5¾ miles (9.2km)
Map: OS Explorer 171 Chiltern Hills West
Start/finish: small parking area in centre of Turville; grid ref SU 767911
Ascent/gradient: 1
Paths: field and woodland paths, some road walking; 9 stiles
Landscape: rolling Chiltern countryside, farmland and woodland

Picturesque cottages in Turville

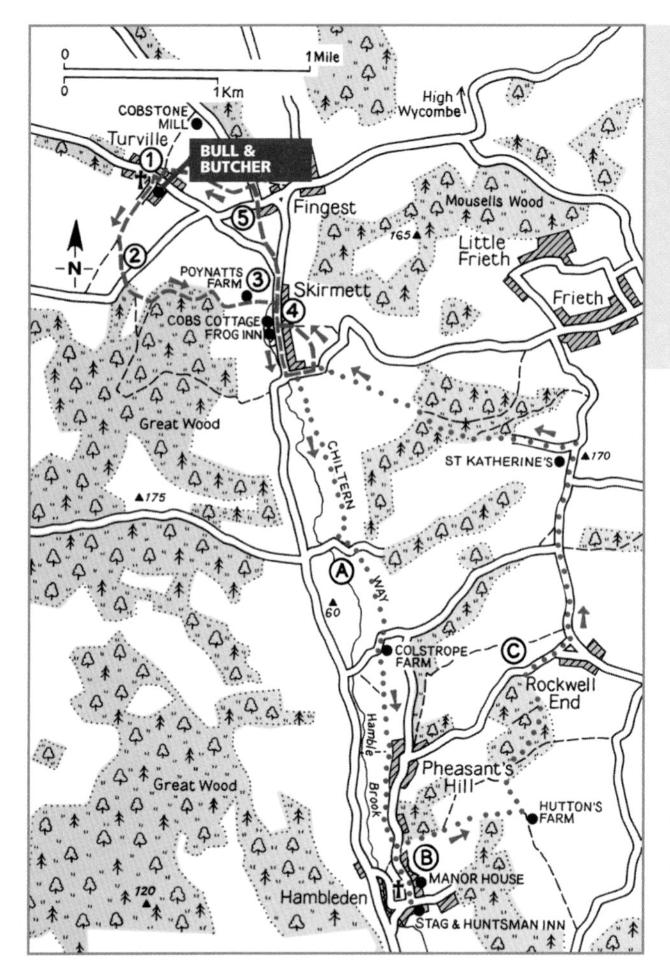

While there

Visit Turville's Church of St Mary the Virgin. There was a church here in the 12th century, but it is not clear if there was one on this site before that. The first vicar of Turville recorded on the roll in the porch was a Benedictine monk who came here from St Albans in 1228. The squat tower dates from about 1340.

Walk directions

❶ Park near the **Bull & Butcher** and take the lane just to the left of the church entrance, with Sleepy Cottage on the corner. Pass Square Close Cottages and the school before continuing on the Chiltern Way through a tunnel of trees. Climb gently to a gate and keep ahead along the field edge to a waymark in the boundary. Branch half-left, heading diagonally down the field to a stile.

❷ Cross the road to a further stile and follow the track through the trees, passing a gas installation on the right. Pass a bench on the left before breaking cover from the trees. Avoid a path branching off to the right and continue up the field slope to the next belt of trees. Turville and its windmill are clearly seen over to the left. Enter the woodland and keep left at the junction. Follow the clear, wide path as it contours round the slopes, with the ground, dotted with beech trees, rippling away to the left. Descend the hillside, keeping to the woodland edge. Follow the fence and bear left at the next corner, heading to a stile by Poynatts Farm.

❸ Walk along the drive to the road, bear right and enter Skirmett. On the right is Cobs Cottage and next door to it is the aptly-named Ramblers. Pass the Frog Inn and follow the road south to the next junction. An assortment of houses, a telephone box and a post box line the route. Turn left, pass a stile on the right (the extension loop starts here) and walk along to the next left footpath. Follow the field edge to a bungalow and stile, cross over to a drive and make for the road.

❹ Bear right, heading out of the village to the junction with Watery Lane. 'Except for access' signs can be seen here now. Look for the stile and footpath immediately to the right of it. Cross the field to a stile in the corner and make for the boundary hedge ahead in the next field. Cross the stile and head diagonally right to a hedge by some houses. Once over the stile, take the road opposite, signposted 'Ibstone and Stokenchurch'.

❺ Walk up the road for about 120 yards (110m) and swing left at the first waymarked junction. Follow the Chiltern Way between trees, with teasing glimpses of the Chilterns themselves. Cross a stile and head diagonally down the field towards Turville. Make for a track and follow it to the village green and back to the pub.

Extension to Hambledon

For a longer loop to pretty Hambledon, near the road junction at the southern end of Skirmett, close to Stud Farm and between Points ❸ and ❹, look for a stile and follow the Chiltern Way, crossing six stiles to reach a house, Point Ⓐ.

Keep to the left of the house and follow the path through the trees. Keep alongside a hedge, heading towards houses. Cross the field and continue on a track. Go straight on at the road, passing Colstrope Farm on the left. Look for a gate on the right bend. Continue ahead to a gate and keep the field edge on your right. Head for a gate and continue, with the field edge now on your left. Make for Pheasant's Hill through several gates. Cross a drive to a gate and continue beside a paddock. Ahead lies a stile and gate. Cross the next field, go through a gate and veer left to another. Swing right on the road into Hambleden.

Like nearby Turville, this has become a favourite with film makers and television producers. The Walt Disney movie *101 Dalmatians* (1996) was filmed here, as were *Sleepy Hollow* (1999) and *The Avengers* (1998). Hambleden was also used in the TV adaptation of Joanna Trollope's novel *A Village Affair* (1989).

Retrace your steps, keeping the church on the left and the manor on the right. At Point Ⓑ pass pairs of cottages and bear right where there is a footpath sign on the left. Follow the track up the hill through the trees, and keep ahead between fields. Pass a stile on the left and continue towards outbuildings at Hutton's Farm. Bear sharp left just before them and cross a stile. Follow the track into woodland. Keep left at the fork, cross a track and continue ahead on a grassy path. Cross a stile and keep right at the road.

At Point Ⓒ walk along to Rockwell End, swing left here and eventually pass a turning on the right for Marlow. Bear left just beyond St Katherine's, a retreat, following the tarmac lane to a house with a balcony. The lane dwindles to a path here and descends gradually between trees and bushes. Pass a path running off sharp right and on reaching the road, keep left. Walk down to the path on the right, skirt the field and rejoin the original walk at Point ❹.

Bull & Butcher

Turville RG9 6QU
Tel: 01491 638283
Directions: *from the M40, junction 5, follow signs for Ibstone; turn right at a T-junction, and the pub is ¼ mile (0.4km) further on*
Open: *11–3, 6–11 (Sat 11–3, 6.30–11; Sun 12–5, 7–10.30)*
Bar meals: *lunch served all week, 12–2; dinner served Mon–Sat, 6–11; average main course £10.95*
Restaurant: *lunch served all week, 12–2; dinner served Mon–Sat, 6–11; average 3 course à la carte £17*
Brewery/company: *Brakspear*
Principal beers: *Brakspear Mild, Bitter, Special, Old & Choice*
Dogs allowed
Parking: *20*

A lovely 16th*-century black-and-white timbered pub tucked away in a secluded valley, in a classic Chiltern village that is regularly used as a film set. It has two unspoilt, low-ceilinged bars with open fires, a welcoming atmosphere, and good restaurant-style food served in a traditional pub setting.*

Daily menus, served throughout, show imagination and flare and make good use of fresh local produce, including local estate game, and fish bought direct from Billingsgate. Don't expect traditional pub food: light meals include salads – grilled goat's cheese salad with tapenade, warm salad of king scallops and wild mushrooms – or starters like hot home-smoked beef pastrami on rye, and smoked haddock, spinach and potato terrine. Hearty, rustic main dishes may feature Toulouse sausages with mash, roast shallots and gravy, and calves' liver with Peccorino mash and smoked bacon. Tip-top Brakspear ales on tap, and 37 wines by the glass.

13: Rambling in the Hampshire countryside

The views from this scenic walk, on the edge of Farley Mount Country Park, are some of the best in Hampshire.

The middle stages of this varied walk are under cover of trees. The route passes through an ancient coppice on the edge Farley Mount Country Park. Extending to 1,000 acres (405ha), the park is a popular amenity area with a wide variety of wildlife. The views over open countryside are outstanding.

Walk directions

❶ From the front of the **Plough Inn** turn left and walk up the road towards Lainston House. At the first junction, turn right and drop down narrow Dean Lane, walking between trees and hedgerows. Pass a path in the right-hand bank. Continue down beyond Dean Hill Cottage to the pretty hamlet of Dean.

❷ As the road bends left by Barn Cottage, go straight on along a bridleway running between hedges and trees. Head up the chalk slope and avoid turnings on the left and right. Keep left at the fork, and now the path runs through a tunnel of yew trees, passing a turning on the right. Continue on the main bridleway all the way to the road.

❸ Turn right and pass a remote house and some barns. Just beyond them the lane becomes enveloped by woodland. Avoid a path running into the trees on the right and make for the second wide entrance to Farley Mount Country Park, also on the right.

❹ Follow the winding track through Crab Wood, all the way to the road. Cross over to two barriers. Take the left one and turn right onto a path after about 50 yards (46m). Keep right at the next fork and then turn right at a

Walk information

Distance: 4 miles (6.4km)
Map: OS Explorer 132 Winchester, New Alresford & East Meon
Start/finish: Plough Inn, Sparsholt; grid ref SU 438314
Ascent/gradient: 2
Paths: bridleways, country roads, woodland tracks and paths
Landscape: remote, unpopulated expanses of wood and downland

Folly in Farley Mount Country Park

crossroads. On reaching a straight track after a few paces, turn left and walk along to a junction. Cross over the track and follow the path, with fencing on the left.

❺ Follow the bridleway as it heads for the north-east boundary of West Wood, passing alongside silver birch trees. Eventually the trees thin, and beside you now are fields and paddocks. After about half a mile (800m) on the bridleway you join a track serving several bungalows.

❻ Just before reaching the road junction, look for a path veering off half-left into the trees. Follow it down to the lane and turn left. Walk back into Sparsholt and return to the **Plough.**

Plough Inn

Main Rd, Sparsholt, nr Winchester SO21 2NW
Tel: 01962 776353
Directions: *from Winchester take B3049 (A272) west; turn left to Sparsholt; the Plough is 1 mile (1.6km) down the lane*
Open: *11–3, 6–11 (Sun 12–3, 6–10.30)*
Bar meals: *lunch and dinner served all week, 12–2, 6–9*
Restaurant: *lunch and dinner served all week, 12–2, 6–9*
Brewery/company: *Wadworth*
Principal beers: *Wadworth Henry's IPA, 6X, Farmers Glory, Old Timer*
Children welcome
Dogs allowed
Parking: *90*

Just 2 miles *(3.2km) from Winchester, this extended 200-year-old cottage located on the edge of the village overlooks open fields from its delightful flower- and shrub-filled garden. Inside you will find a bustling bar with pine tables, its beams garlanded with dried hops, an open log fire, and a decent selection of wines and real ales from Wadworth. Original cottage front rooms are particularly conducive to intimate dining and extensive blackboard menus offer imaginative home-cooked food.*

At lunchtime expect 'doorstep' sandwiches and locally made speciality sausages, served in a comfortable atmosphere devoid of juke box or fruit machines. Lunchtimes can get very busy and booking is definitely advised for the evening session. Representative dishes might include pan-fried marlin with a gâteau of vegetables and herb oil, sautéed lambs' liver and bacon with mash and onion gravy, or teriyaki chicken breast with mango on a sweet pepper stir fry. Nursery puddings include fruit crumbles, with British cheeses as a popular alternative.

Walk information

Distance: 3 miles (4.8km) + extension 4¼ miles (6.8 km)
Map: OS Explorer 133 Haslemere & Petersfield
Start/finish: by village green in Hawkley; grid ref SU 746291
Ascent/gradient: 2
Paths: field and woodland paths, rutted, wet and muddy tracks (in winter) and short stretches of road; 29 stiles
Landscape: rolling, beech-clad hills, a hidden, flower-filled valley and undulating farmland

The view from Shoulder of Mutton Hill

14: On the trail of an English poet

A walk around the village of Hawkley extends on to Steep, and the extraordinary, timeless Harrow Inn.

William Cobbett wrote 'beautiful beyond description' in his Rural Rides, after passing through Hawkley in 1822 on his way from East Meon to Thursley. In common with other famous people who lived in and wrote about this area. Cobbett was enchanted by the rolling, beech-clad hills that characterise this relatively unexplored part of Hampshire. Known locally as 'hangers', from the Anglo-Saxon hangra meaning 'sloping wood', these fine beech woods cling to the steep chalk escarpment that links Selborne to Steep. Many have charming names such as Happersnapper Hanger and Strawberry Hanger.

Poet Edward Thomas lived at Steep from 1906 to his death in 1917. His abiding love for the beech hangers, mysterious combes and the sheer beauty of the landscape inspired him to write some of his finest poems, including 'Up in the Wind', 'The New House' and 'Wind and Mist'. You, too, will be find the views breathtaking as you dip and climb through the hangers to the summit of Shoulder of Mutton Hill, Thomas's favoured spot above his beloved Steep.

The walk begins from Hawkley, tucked away beneath Hawkley Hanger. You descend into the lush meadows of the Oakshott Valley, before a steep ascent on an old droving track to the top of Mutton Hill. Here, in a tranquil glade on its higher slopes, you will find a sarsen stone dedicated to Edward Thomas. With such surprising views across Steep and of 'sixty miles of South Downs at one glance', as Thomas described it, it is no wonder that he loved this area. Inscribed on the stone is an apt line from one of his poems, 'and I rose up and knew I was tired and continued my journey'.

The return walk joins the Hangers Way, a 21-mile (33.6km) long distance trail traversing east Hampshire from Queen Elizabeth Country Park to Alton.

Walk directions

❶ With your back to Hawkley church, walk left beside the green to the road junction. With the Hawkley Inn away to your left, cross straight over down Cheesecombe Farm Lane, signed 'the Hangers Way'. Shortly, bear off right along a concrete path. Descend to a stile and keep straight on at the fork of paths,

Look for

Two memorials in All Saints Church at Steep are worth looking for. One is to Basil Marsden who was killed in an avalanche in the Andes in 1928; the other is to a Martha Legg who died in 1829 at the remarkable age of 105. The nearby River Ashford was once powerful enough to drive a fulling mill and later a grain mill. You can see the old mill and its waterfall just before you get to Ashford Chace.

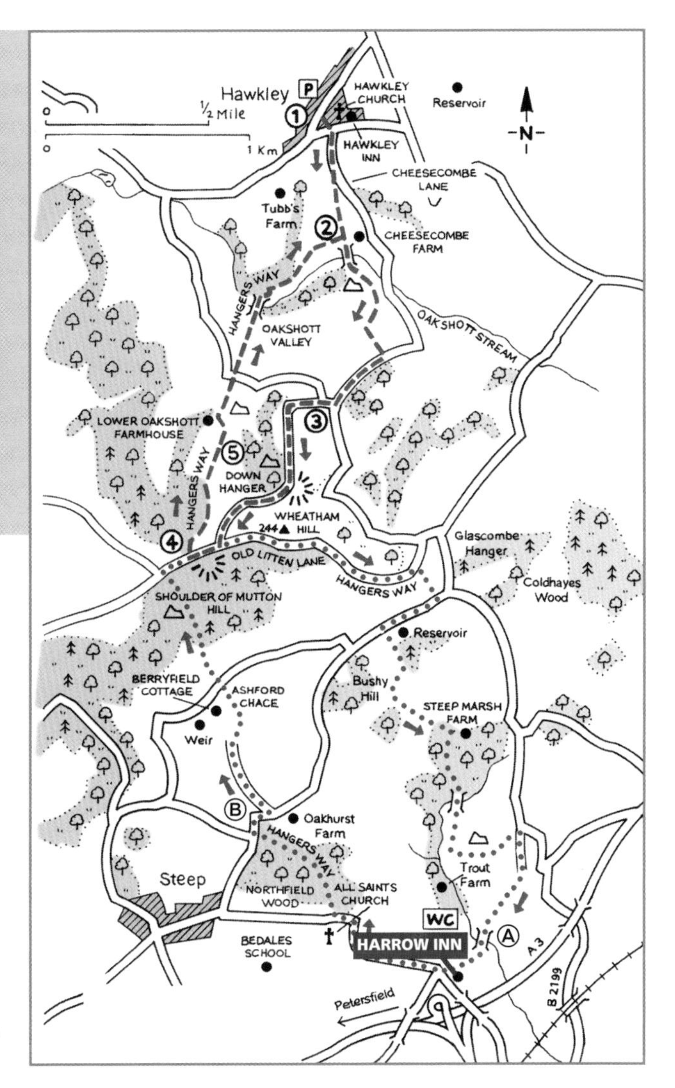

with Cheesecombe Farm to the left.

2 Cross Oakshott Stream and keep left along the field edge beside woodland. Steeply ascend to a stile, keep right to a further stile, then turn left beside the fence and drop down to a track. Turn right, to reach a lane, then right again for 55 yards (50m) to take the waymarked right of way beside Wheatham Hill House.

3 Climb the long and steep, chalky track up through Down Hanger (this gets very wet and muddy), with views east along the South Downs unfolding. At the top of Wheatham Hill, turn right at a T-junction of tracks along Old Litten Lane. In 300 yards (274m), take the Hangers Way right over a stile. For the Edward Thomas memorial stone and magnificent South Downs views, continue along the track for 200 yards (183m) and turn left with a waymarker. Pass beside the wooden barrier and drop down to the clearing on Shoulder of Mutton Hill.

4 Follow the Hangers Way as it descends through the edge of beech woods and steeply down across lush meadowland, eventually joining the drive to Lower Oakshott Farmhouse and a road.

5 Turn right, then left over the stile and follow the defined Hangers Way path through the Oakshott Valley, crossing stiles, plank bridges and meadows to reach the junction of paths before

Harrow Inn

Steep GU32 2DA
Tel: 01730 262685
Directions: *Turn off A3 onto the A272, go left through Sheet, take the road opposite the church and go over the A3 bypass bridge*
Open: *12–2.30, 6–11 (Sat 11–3, 6–11; Sun 12–3, 7–10.30)*
Bar meals: *lunch and dinner served all week, 12–2, 7–9; average main course £7*
Brewery/company: *free house*
Principal beers: *Ringwood Best, Cheriton Diggers Gold & Pots Ale, Ballards Best*
Dogs allowed
Parking: *15*

This gem of *a rustic pub has been run by the McCutchen family since 1929. Totally unspoilt, it is tucked away down a sleepy lane that was once the drovers' route from Liss to Petersfield. Today the tile-hung 500-year-old building is a popular watering hole with hikers following the Hanger's Way, who stop to enjoy the delightful cottage garden.*

The two character bars, each with scrubbed wooden tables, boarded walls and seasonal flower arrangements, are the perfect environment to relax over a decent pint of local ale. This gives an opportunity to contemplate choices of smoked salmon sandwiches, ploughman's lunches and maybe Stilton and broccoli quiche, followed by treacle tart or chocolate nut biscuits, all cooked in the long-serving Rayburn. Little has changed over the years – and why should it? A true survivor, the Harrow remains resistant to change.

Cheesecombe Farm. Turn left to the stile and retrace your steps back to Hawkley.

Extension to Steep

On top of Wheatham Hill, follow the rutted track left for ½ mile (800m) downhill through the Ashford Hangers. Just before a lane, climb the stile right and descend through an avenue of trees to a stile and lane. Turn right then, in 400 yards (366m), take the footpath left. Descend to a stile and bear right around the field edge to a stile by woodland. Turn right beside the fence and keep left along the field edge to Steep Marsh Farm.

Turn right beside sheds and join a wooded track. Shortly, cross the drive and lawn to a house back into woodland. Cross a stream (Point Ⓐ) and, just before reaching a metalled drive, climb the steep path left beside trees to a stile. Turn left around the field edge to a track and follow it to a lane. Turn right then, at a sharp left bend, bear off right into woodland. Walk above a deep ditch and past timbered cottages to a footbridge. Continue ahead and pass the **Harrow Inn.** Turn right at the junction and walk uphill into Steep to All Saints Church.

The partly-Norman church lies close to Bedales School, which first attracted Thomas to the village in 1906, so that his children could attend the school. There's a memorial window to the poet by Lawrence Whistler (1912–2000) in the church.

Follow the Hangers Way opposite, across a playing field and down through Northfield Wood to a stile. Walk along the left-hand field edge to a stile and road, Point Ⓑ. Turn right then, as it swings right, keep ahead up the footpath (the waterfall is to your left). At a junction, turn left and walk through woodland to join a drive leading to a lane beside Ashford Chace.

Thomas lived in three houses in the village. You'll find Berryfield Cottage, the poet's first home, next to Ashford Chace. Turn right, then almost immediately left along a footpath towards Shoulder of Mutton Hill. Keep right at a fork to climb steeply up the grassy scarp slope to the memorial stone. At the top, keep ahead to a track. Turn right, then in 200yds (183m) turn left to rejoin the main walk at Point ❹.

While there

Track down the White Horse, close to Froxfield and Priors Dean on the unclassified road from Petersfield to the A32. One of the highest and most isolated pubs in Hampshire, it's another classic example of an unspoilt country pub and was a regular haunt of Edward Thomas – his tankard still hangs in the bar. The pub inspired his first poem, 'Up in the Wind', written in 1914 and describing the inn's isolation. It begins with the lines *'I could wring the old thing's neck that put it there! A public-house'.*

15: Sea views on the Isle of Wight

With its many miles of footpaths, well signposted trails and stunning scenery, the Isle of Wight is perfect for walking.

Walk information

Distance: 4 miles (6.4 km)
Map: OS Outdoor Leisure 29 Isle of Wight
Start/finish: Seaview Hotel, Seaview; grid ref SZ 629917
Ascent/gradient: 1
Paths: coastal path, bridleways, footpaths, some road walking
Landscape: country and urban areas

A sunny day at Bembridge harbour

This varied route follows the Barnsley Trail though open countryside from the picturesque sailing village of Seaview. It is one of the island's best-loved spots, and the jewel in its crown has to be the **Seaview Hotel**, a pub-cum-restaurant built in 1795.

Walk directions

❶ From the **Seaview Hotel** turn left towards the seafront. Keep the shoreline on your right and follow the Isle of Wight Coastal Path towards Ryde. As the trail rejoins the main road on a bend, turn left, pass Bluett Avenue and turn right at the junction with Fairey Road. Follow the track to meet the B3330 at Nettlestone Hill.

❷ Turn right, through the Barnsley Valley, and take the first track on the left, as the road swings to the right. This rural stretch through the valley has an intriguing story. Originally the sea reached as far inland as the Park and Longlands copses, and this type of inlet was greatly favoured by the Romans. During the medieval period the inlet developed into Barnsley Harbour, and although it was prone to silting, like most of the creeks along the north shore of the

island, there was sufficient depth to allow larger ships to sail up to the mill just south of the B3330. The mill pond banks are still visible.

3 Follow the bridleway through the fields to Park Farm. Just before the farm, veer left to join a footpath running through the fields to meet up with the B3330 again. Cross over into Priory Drive and follow it along to the Coastal Path. Turn left, following the trail back to Seaview and the hotel.

4 This final stretch allows you access to St Helen's Duver, a slender spit protruding into Bembridge Harbour. National Trust land, this peaceful haven of grassland, sand dunes and rare flowers can boast more than 200 species of wild plants, including tree lupin, evening primrose and sea thrift. Near by is the ruined tower of St Helen's Church. It was once a priory, and all but the tower has been ravaged by the sea over the centuries.

Seaview Hotel & Restaurant

High St, Seaview, Isle of Wight PO34 5EX
Tel: 01983 612711
Directions: *from B3330 Ryde–Seaview, turn left via Puckpool along seafront (Duver Rd); hotel is on left-hand side*
Open: *11–2.30, 6–11*
Bar meals: *lunch and dinner served all week, 12–2, 7–9.30; average main course £8.95*
Restaurant: *lunch and dinner served all week, 12–2, 7.30–9.30; average 3 course à la carte £25*
Brewery/company: *free house*
Principal beers: *Goddards, Greene King Abbot Ale*
Children welcome
Dogs allowed
Parking: *12*
Rooms: *16 bedrooms en suite from s£55, d£70*

There are stunning *views from here across the sea to Portsmouth naval dockyard. Both navies – merchant and royal – are commemorated in the fascinating collection of artefacts displayed throughout the pub and the different restaurants, including classic ship models, letters from the ill-fated* Titanic, *and bills from the* Queen Mary.

Amid this homage to the sea is another tribute, this time to the fish and seafood freshly caught and brought to the table by local fishermen. Skate wing with lemon and caper noisette, fillet of brill, and monkfish tail are likely to appear on the restaurant menu, along with loin of island pork, and breast of corn-fed chicken stuffed with wild mushrooms and spinach. From the bar menu expect hot crab ramekin, smoked duck breast salad, and braised lamb shank.

16: A short hike around historic Hever

This pleasant walk passes close to historic Hever Castle, in Tudor times the home of the Boleyn family.

Hever Castle later became the property of tycoon William Waldorf Astor, who spent a fortune restoring it. He also built the village of Hever, in Tudor style.

Walk directions

❶ With the **Castle Inn** behind you and St Mary's Church on your right, take the road skirting the lake, keeping Chiddingstone Castle away to your left. Go over Gilwyns crossroads and straight ahead along the undulating road for about ½ mile (800m).

❷ When the road turns sharp left, go through an opening in the fence on your right to a path cutting through the grounds of Hever Castle. The path runs alongside a fence, next to a wood, with a private road to your left. Cross the road by a picturesque rustic bridge and continue between fences to a path crossing Hever churchyard to a lychgate. Noted for its slender spire, the church contains the tomb of Sir Thomas Bullen, father of Anne Boleyn. Anne became Henry VIII's mistress and later, tragically, his second of six wives.

❸ Make for the lychgate and turn left. When the road bends sharp right by the Henry VIII Inn, continue straight ahead via a path, passing the village school on your left. Follow the path to a

Walk information

Distance: 4½ miles (7.2km)
Map: OS Explorer 147 Sevenoaks & Tonbridge
Start/finish: Castle Inn, Chiddingstone; grid ref TQ 500451
Ascent/gradient: 2
Paths: roads, paths (sometimes muddy) and tracks; 2 stiles
Terrain: woodland and farmland

The old moat at Hever Castle

Castle Inn

Chiddingstone TN8 7AH
Tel: 01892 870247
Directions: *south of the B2027 between Tonbridge and Edenbridge*
Open: *11–11*
Bar meals: *lunch and dinner served all week, 12–2, 7.30–9.30*
Restaurant: *lunch served Wed–Mon, 12–2; dinner served all week, 7.30–9.30; average 3 course à la carte £20*
Brewery/company: *free house*
Principal beers: *Larkins Traditional, Harveys Sussex, Young's Ordinary*
Children welcome
Dogs allowed

The Castle Inn *is reputed to have been named in honour of Anne Boleyn, who lived at nearby Hever Castle, but its roots go back much further than that. Nowadays its picturesque mellow brick exterior is a much-used film set –* The Wicked Lady *(1983) and* Room With a View *(1986) were shot here. In 1420 the inn was known as Waterslip House, and it was licensed to sell ale in about 1730, when it became known as the Five Bells. Inside it is full of nooks and crannies, period furniture and evocative curios, with the rambling beamed bar having been remodelled carefully to preserve its unique character. The same family owners have dispensed traditional ales for nearly 40 years, including Larkins Traditional which is brewed at nearby Larkins Farm.*

The inn is also well known for its food. Typical pub food is available, including open sandwiches, ploughman's and filled jacket potatoes, and more substantial dishes like chilli con carne, and chicken curry. However, you will not find chips in any form on this menu. Moving up a few notches there is the Fireside Menu, offering the likes of ham hock and black pudding, or wild mushroom and Cashel Blue cheese tartlet, followed by chargrilled tuna on crushed lobster potatoes, or roasted rump of lamb on a root vegetable purée. Typical sweets might include bitter chocolate tart with Amaretto ice cream, and pistachio and lemon grass crème brûlée. A selection of award-winning British cheeses is always on offer. In the small restaurant these dishes, and more, are on offer, with a serious selection of wines to match – including fine clarets – and an extensive choice of malt whiskies.

quiet road and turn left. On reaching a junction, turn left over a stile and continue by a hedge. Turn right, skirt a wood and continue by a hedge to a stile. Cross it, passing woodland on the right to reach the private road encountered early in the walk.

4 Don't join the road; instead turn right and follow a path alongside a fence. Cross the next road to a gate and go straight ahead between fences along the field edge. Turn right on reaching a wood, then sharp left, over a small footbridge and continue up a steep path.

5 When the path reaches a track, turn left – if it is muddy here, then take the parallel track on the left. Pass alongside a half-timbered house called Withers and turn left down the road. Follow it for about ½ mile (800m) to reach Gilwyns crossroads again. Turn right and return to the **Castle Inn.**

17: Secrets of Friday Street

A walk to Surrey's prettiest and most remote hamlet.

Walk information

Distance: 4 miles (8.4km) + extension 1¼ miles (2km)
Map: OS Explorer 146 Dorking, Box Hill & Reigate
Start/finish: woodland parking at Starveall Corner; grid ref TQ 130432
Ascent/gradient: 2
Paths: easily woodland tracks, but poor waymarking; many stiles
Landscape: thickly wooded sandstone heaths

Friday Street's most famous son is an enigmatic figure who blends life and legend with the effortless ease of King Arthur. There's no denying Stephan Langton's place in the history books. He was born around 1150, and orphaned by the age of ten. His parents may have come from Lincolnshire, though legend has it that he was born in Friday Street.

It's clear that Stephan was educated by monks, but although one source has him singing in the local choir, it seems that he also studied at the University of Paris. Here, it's said, he established himself as a leading theologian; indeed, he would go on to become Archbishop of Canterbury.

By the time he was 18, Stephan was living in Albury, just a few miles down the road from Friday Street. Here he fell in love with Alice, and legend has it that the couple were strolling in the nearby woods when they were set upon by King John and his followers. There's a problem with the story here, since John was by now about 12 months old, and didn't come to the throne for another 30 years. But it's a good story.

John kidnapped Alice, and took her off to his hunting lodge at Tangley, near Guildford. Stephan followed the trail and set fire to the house in an attempt to rescue his sweetheart but, in the confusion, the girl fainted or was overcome by smoke. Thinking her

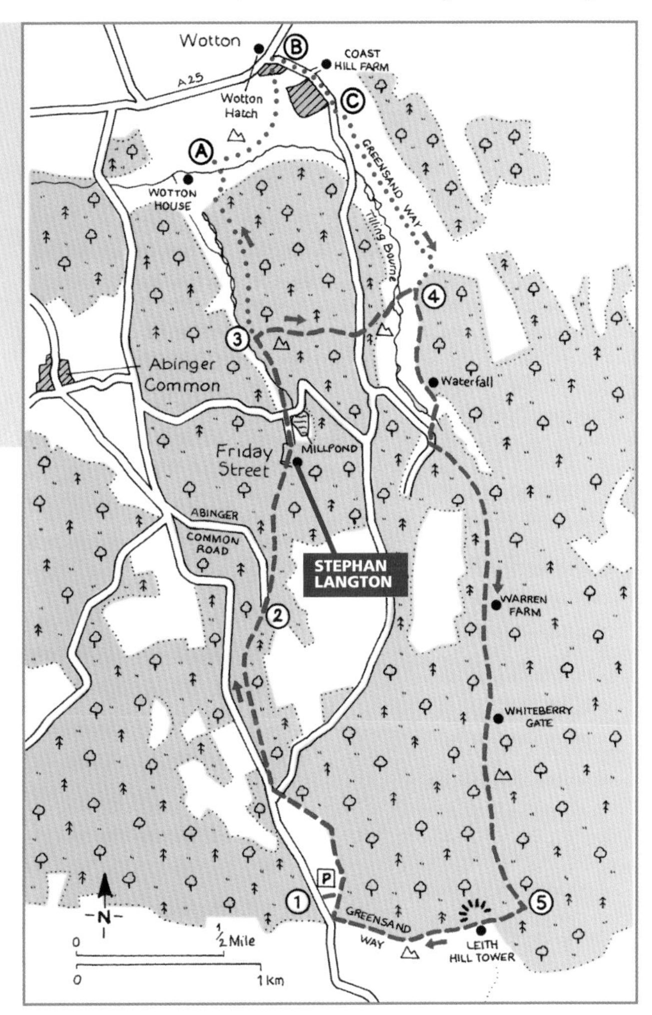

dead, Stephan wandered off to become a monk.

By the dawn of the 13th century, we're back on firmer ground. Not without reason, the idle and self-centred King John was deeply unpopular. He refused to accept Stephan Langton as the Pope's choice of Archbishop of Canterbury, provoking six years of conflict with Rome and the threat of a French invasion. By 1214 the King had capitulated, but he now faced a baronial revolt. Langton stepped in as mediator; he was prominent in drafting the Magna Carta, and was amongst the signatories at Runnymede in 1215.

Meanwhile, Alice recovered from her ordeal and went on to become Abbess of St Catherine's in Guildford. Some years later, the couple were unexpectedly reunited after Mass at St Martha's Chapel near Guildford. But don't expect a happy ending – the Abbess was so overcome with emotion that she died in Stephan's arms.

Walk directions

❶ Leave the car park at the gate near the top left-hand corner. After 45 yards (41m), turn left onto a woodland path and follow it to a crossroads. Turn left and drop down to a road junction. Take the road towards Abinger Common and Wotton; then, 90 yards (82m) further on, turn onto the narrow, unsignposted path on your right. Cross a tarmac drive, and continue as it widens into a woodland ride.

❷ Leave the woods and continue briefly along Abinger Common Road. When you reach a house called St John's, fork right onto the bridleway and follow it through to Friday Street. Pass the **Stephan Langton** pub and the millpond, and drop down past the letter box at Pond Cottage. Follow the rough track towards Wotton, bear left past Yew Tree Cottage, and continue to a gate. (The Wotton extension starts here.)

❸ Turn right over the stile, and climb the sandy track into the woods. Soon it levels off, bears left past a young plantation, then veers right at the far end. Two stiles carry you across Sheephouse Lane, and soon you're dropping to another stile. Nip over, and follow the fence across the Tilling Bourne until you reach two steps up to a stile.

❹ Cross the stile, and turn right onto the Greensand Way. It brushes the road at the Triple Bar Riding Centre then turns left onto a public bridleway. Keep right at the National Trust's Henman Base Camp, and right again at Warren Farm, where the forest road ends. Here the waymarked Greensand Way forks right again, along the narrow woodland track. Keep ahead when you come to the bench and three-way signpost at Whiteberry Gate, climbing steadily at first, then more steeply, until you come to a barrier and five-way junction.

❺ The way ahead dives steeply down; turn right, still following the waymarked Greensand Way as it pushes up towards Leith Hill Tower. Pass the tower, taking the left-hand fork towards Starveall Corner. Follow the broad track back to the barrier at Leith Hill Road, then swing right onto the signposted bridleway. After 140yds (128m), turn left for the last little stretch back to the car park.

Extension to Wotton

The diarist John Evelyn was born in Wotton House in 1620, and you'll get some good views of the house and grounds on this walk. But there was more to the man than his diary, which wasn't published until more than a century after his death. He trained as a lawyer and was a friend of

Look for

Shortly after you join the Greensand Way you'll see an impressive waterfall on your left, cascading 65 feet (20m) into a pool. It's fed by a leat from Brookmill Pond and was built around 1738 as part of an ambitious landscaping project.

While there

In return for climbing the 75 spiral steps of Leith Hill Tower you'll get a view that stretches from the London Eye to the coast. It was built in 1766 by Richard Hull of Leith Hill Place it's popularly believed he wanted to raise the 967-foot (295-m) hill to exactly 1,000 feet (305m). After his death in 1772, he was buried beneath its floor. During the next hundred years the tower was raised to its present height of 1,029 feet (329m). The National Trust took over in 1923, and has an information room on the first floor.

Samuel Pepys. In his own lifetime, Evelyn was best known for his book *Sylva, or a Discourse of Forest Trees*. His interests included architecture and gardening; he was involved in landscaping the family estates at Wotton, and also helped to plan the gardens at nearby Albury Park. Towards the end of his life he returned to Wotton and lived with his brother. He inherited the estate in 1699, and died in 1706.

Leave the main walk at Point ❸, and carry straight on over the stile beside the gate. The vistas are more open as you approach Wotton House and, for company, an attractive chain of ornamental pools runs though the valley less than 100 yards (91m) from the track.

The route narrows as you approach Wotton House, then swings to the right and drops down to a footpath crossroads. Keep straight on, down the narrowest of the paths, then nip over the stile and follow the field edge to a second stile, Point Ⓐ. Look to the left here for some good views of Wotton House. Cross the stile onto the drive to Wotton House, turn right, and climb steadily to a large 'Private' notice. Here you must leave the drive, jump the stile on your right, and bear left across the field. Nip over the stile at the far side, and follow the right of way through the Wotton Hatch car park to the A25 junction with Damphurst Lane, Point Ⓑ.

Turn right into Damphurst Lane. After 285 yards (260m), you'll reach the entrance to Coast Hill Farm. Turn in to the left, and follow the waymarked footpath that runs alongside the road until you reach a lodge cottage, Point Ⓒ. Walk up the cottage drive and, after 40 yards (37m), fork left onto the waymarked Greensand Way. Now, simply follow the track until you rejoin the main route at Point ❹.

Stephan Langton

Friday Street, Abinger Common RH5 6RJ
Tel: 01306 730775
Directions: *between Dorking and Guildford leave A25 at Hollow Lane, west of Wotton; go south for 1½ miles (2.4km) then left into Friday Street*
Open: *11–3, 6–11 (summer weekends all day)*
Bar meals: *lunch served Tue–Sun, 12.30–3; dinner served Tue–Sat, 7–10; average main course £10*
Restaurant: *lunch served Tue–Sun, 12.30–3; dinner served Tue–Sat, 7–10; average 3 course à la carte £19*
Brewery/company: *free house*
Principal beers: *Fuller's London Pride, Adnams*
Children welcome
Dogs allowed
Parking: *20*

***A lovely brick**-and-timber inn, named after the 13th-century Archbishop of Canterbury and local boy. Although it looks much older, and was built on the site of another inn, this secluded hostelry only dates back to 1930. Some of Surrey's loveliest walks are found near by.*

The pub is being gradually refurbished to match Jonathan Coomb's upmarket food. The bar choice includes duck confit with Puy lentils and spring greens, and Moroccan-style braised lamb, while the dinner menu offers a short but well balanced choice: chargrilled squid with chilli and rocket, seared marlin niçoise, and buttermilk pudding with poached rhubarb is a typical meal.

18: Following a cycle route by the Mawddach estuary

An outstanding linear walk leads along the banks of the Mawddach Estuary, following the route of the defunct Great Western Railway.

The trail, offering some of the best views in Wales, runs in front of the hotel along the sea wall. Considered by many to be Europe's most beautiful estuary, this breathtaking corner of the country inspired poets such as William Wordsworth and Gerard Manley Hopkins.

Walk directions

❶ Turn left out of the front door of the handsome old **George III Hotel** and head for the sea. The trail is easy to follow, and a ½-mile (800-m) extension at the

Walk information

Distance: Any distance up to 14 miles (22.5km)
Map: OS Landranger 23 Cadair Idris & Llyn Tegid
Start/finish: George III Hotel, Penmaenpool; grid ref SH 693184
Ascent/gradient: 2
Paths: footpath, cycle trail; suitable for wheelchairs but a little rough at 3-miles (4.8km)
Landscape: flat trail by estuary; 7 miles (11.3km) are vehicle free

Low tide on the Mawddach estuary

George III Hotel

Penmaenpool, Dolgellau
LL40 1YD
Tel: 01341 422525
Directions: *2 miles (3.2km) west of Dolgellau on A493, beyond RSPB Centre*
Open: *11–11*
Bar meals: *Lunch and dinner served all week, 12–2.30, 6.30–9.30; average main course £8*
Restaurant: *lunch served Sunday, 12–2; dinner all week, 7–9; average 3 course à la carte £27.50*
Brewery/company: *free house*
Principle beers: *Ruddles Best, John Smith's Cask, Directors*
Children welcome
Dogs allowed
Parking: *60*
Rooms: *11 bedrooms en suite from s£45, d£80*

At the edge *of the magnificent Mawddach Estuary, and with splendid views to the Snowdonia National Park, the hotel stands a mile or so outside town, in tranquil waterside meadows inhabited by swans, herons and otters. Part of the accommodation is housed in a former railway station. The Cellar Bar beside the water is ideal for families, cyclists and walkers, while the upper level Dresser Bar, with an unusual bar counter from which it is named, and the main dining rooms are rather more genteel. Noted for local salmon and sea trout, pheasant and wild duck in season, meals are home-cooked by the landlord. At one end of the scale are bar snacks including soups, chicken liver pâté, and steak and Stilton baps, while the restaurant weighs in with starters such as crêpe de crevettes, followed perhaps by poached cod loin on spinach with mornay sauce, or best end of Welsh lamb roasted and served with broad beans, silverskin onions and a red wine and rosemary sauce.*

Morning coffee and afternoon tea are available, and food can be served outside on the terrace.

end can be added if you continue across the Barmouth railway bridge. Note that there is a charge for crossing the wooden bridge, built in 1865. Small rock promontories jutting out into the river are a feature of the estuary, and benches offer the chance to rest before continuing with the walk or turning round and returning to the **George III**.

❷ The trail occasionally passes through a Sustrans gate; these are wide enough for wheelchairs, and easy for bicycles. The trail is now a fully recognised Sustrans cycle route, but still remains an official long distance footpath mostly maintained by Sustrans grants and the Snowdonia National Park. Look out for RSPB-protected woodlands and wetlands, as well as one of the largest reedbeds in Wales. The river here is home to a variety of birds, including oystercatchers, herons, shellducks, mallards and curlews. The estuary is also renowned for its salmon, sea trout, bass and mullet. The mountain of Cader Idris stands out to your right, and the disused slate mines at Arthog are also visible. Rhododendrons are seen in the oak woodland around the river, particularly striking when in full bloom.

❸ When you have walked far enough, simply retrace your steps to return to the pub.

19: Hills and history at Llanvair Discoed

This delightful circular walk explores the attractive rolling countryside to the north of Llanvair Discoed.

The name Llanvair Discoed means 'church under the wood'.

Walk directions

❶ On leaving the **Woodland Restaurant and Bar**, take Well Lane, the narrow road to the left, and follow it uphill. Look out for the village well in the right boundary. Just beyond it, on the left, are the renovated buildings of a farm. New farm barns have also been built on the right-hand side of the lane.

❷ Continue to where Well Lane terminates and you will see Slade's Cottage, which has been enlarged over the years and was once a small dwelling. Look for a

Walk information

Distance: 2¼ miles (3.6km)
Map: OS Explorer OL 14 Wye Valley & Forest of Dean
Start/finish: Woodland Restaurant, Llanvair Discoed; grid ref SO 447923
Ascent/gradient: 1
Paths: footpaths, bridleways and country roads; 2 stiles
Landscape: rolling hills and farmland

Right: view over valley
Below: a Roman remnant at Caerwent

stile and gate just beyond the cottage. Cross over and turn immediately right, passing over a stream. Keep ahead up the field, with the fence and trees to your right.

❸ As you begin to approach the top right-hand corner of the field, head towards a large tree near a gap in the stone wall. Pass through the gap, cross the stile and follow the path, keeping a thatched cottage to your right. Just beyond the cottage, which was recently renovated as part of a medieval village restoration programme, you reach a junction of paths. Turn left here and follow the route of a pleasant woodland path.

❹ Cross a stile and continue ahead until you reach a junction with a bridleway skirting the bottom of Gray Hill. Turn left here and head down the metalled road towards Llanvair Discoed. Turn left at the next junction and walk downhill to return to the **Woodland Restaurant and Bar**. Along here you can see the remains of Llanvair Castle, located within the grounds of a private house. Below lies the local church, which is worth a closer inspection.

Woodland Restaurant & Bar

Llanvair Discoed NP16 6LX
Tel: 01633 400313
Open: *11–3, 6–11 (Sun 12–3, 7–10.30)*
Bar meals: *lunch served all week, 12–2; dinner served Mon–Sat, 6.30–10; average main course £11.25*
Restaurant: *lunch served all week, 12–2; dinner served Mon–Sat, 6.30–9.30; average 3 course à la carte £23*
Brewery/company: *free house*
Principal beers: *Buckley's Best, Reverend James, Somerset & Dorset, H.B.*
Children welcome
Dogs allowed
Parking: *30*

An old inn, *extended to accommodate a growing number of diners, the Woodland is located close to the Roman fortress town of Caerwent and Wentworth's forest and reservoir. It remains at heart a friendly village local, serving a good range of beers.*

A varied menu of freshly prepared dishes caters for all tastes, from ciabatta bread with various toppings to Welsh lamb loin wrapped in spinach and filo pastry on a bed of wild mushroom and rosemary risotto. Meat is sourced from a local butcher, who slaughters all his own meat, and the fish is mostly from Cornwall – maybe sea bass cooked in rock salt and lemon.

Outside there's a large, well equipped garden with plenty of bench seating.

20: Brechfa Pool, a Brecon beauty spot

Enjoy a longer walk from a splendid old pub in the Brecon Beacons National Park.

Walk information

Distance: 7 miles (11.6km)
Map: OS Outdoor Leisure 13 Brecon Beacons National Park
Start/finish: Griffin Inn, Llyswen; grid ref SO 132379
Ascent/gradient: 2
Paths: riverside and woodland paths, grass; short, steep descent to finish, may be slippery
Landscape: riverside stretches and hillside walking

The mansion of Langoed Castle, Llyswen

The route offers a ramble through contrasting Wye Valley landscapes from a sheltered, shady stretch along the delightful River Wye, to the open, invigorating area around the slopes of Mynydd Forest. Finally, the walk takes in Brechfa Pool with its magnificent views of the Black Mountains and the Brecon Beacons.

Walk directions

❶ From the **Griffin Inn** make for the church in Llyswen. On leaving it, turn right along the A470 to reach Bridge End Inn. Turn right, then just before the river bridge (Boughrood Bridge) bear left along a metalled lane by the Wye. Continue ahead on a riverside path for over a mile (1.6km), until reaching the main A470 at Trericket Mill.

❷ Turn right along the road for about 100 yards (91m), then go left up a farm road. Climb past the first farm, then at the next, bear left around the barn and shortly turn left down a path by a wall, veering left down to the river. Cross a footbridge and head up the bank opposite, then bear left past a house on the right. After 100 yards (91m) go through a gate to the road.

❸ Turn right, re-passing the house, and proceed uphill to a

Griffin Inn

Llyswen, Brecon LD3 0UR
Tel: 01874 754241
Directions: *On A470 Brecon–Builth Wells road*
Open: *10.30–3, 6–11 (summer 11–11)*
Bar meals: *Lunch and dinner served all week, 12–2, 7–9. Average main course £6.95*
Restaurant: *Lunch and dinner served all week, 12–2, 7–9; average 3 course à la carte £15*
Brewery/company: *S A Brain*
Principle beers: *Brains Reverend James, SA, Arms Park, Buckleys Best & Smooth*
Dogs allowed
Parking: *20*

A family-run favourite *for some 17 years, this lovely ivy-covered inn provides a relaxed atmosphere, traditional comforts and all the sporting benefits of a stay in the glorious Wye Valley. It's a hub of the local community, so guests could find themselves engaged in conversation with the local poacher, preacher, the publicans themselves or even the village bobby. On a summer's day, sit outside and watch the world go by. In winter, take refuge in one of the cosy public rooms: perhaps the bar, with its huge open fire, bare tiled floor and fishing memorabilia, or the lounge with its charming mixture of chairs and sofas clustered around a log-burning stove, or the dining room, an equally rustic affair with bare beams and blackboard menus.*

Wye salmon, fresh trout and seasonal game, fruit and vegetables all play their part in the array of home-cooked produce. At lunch or dinner choose from dishes such as rack of Welsh lamb, Mediterranean chicken, Welsh black beef daube, and Exmoor steak (fillet steak stuffed with Stilton, wrapped in bacon and set on a Stilton and port sauce). An impressive array of fresh fish direct from Cornwall could include sea bass, sole, lobster or scallops. Desserts are all home-made and might include trifle, bread-and-butter pudding or mango crème brûlée. Those who fancy a lighter lunch can opt for sandwiches, baguettes or a ploughman's.

fork. Keep left, then, where the lane bends right, take a grassy path on the left, running almost parallel with the lane, to reach a gate and boundary wall. Follow the wall along and round to a further gate, then continue up the track, which veers right to reach the open moor.

❹ After about ½ mile (0.8km) the track divides into three; take the middle arm so that the boundary wall, still visible, gradually gets nearer. Continue to a minor road, turn right and head for Brechfa Pool and a small chapel. The pool was a favourite with the 19th-century rector Francis Kilvert, whose diary of rural life in this area became a minor classic. Kilvert was vicar at Bredwardine until his early death in 1879. Go round the pool clockwise, then turn left along a broad, grassy swathe to reach a lane.

❺ Cross a cattle-grid, then when the lane bends right, continue ahead following a steeply descending bridleway to the main road. Bear left and return to the **Griffin** at Llyswen.

Walk information

Distance: $4\frac{1}{2}$ miles (7.2km)
Map: OS Explorer 216 Welshpool and Montgomery
Start/finish: car park on Bishops Castle Street at south end of town; grid ref SJ 224963
Ascent/gradient: 2
Paths: well defined paths, farm tracks and country lanes; 3 stiles
Landscape: pastoral hills overlooking wide plains of the Severn

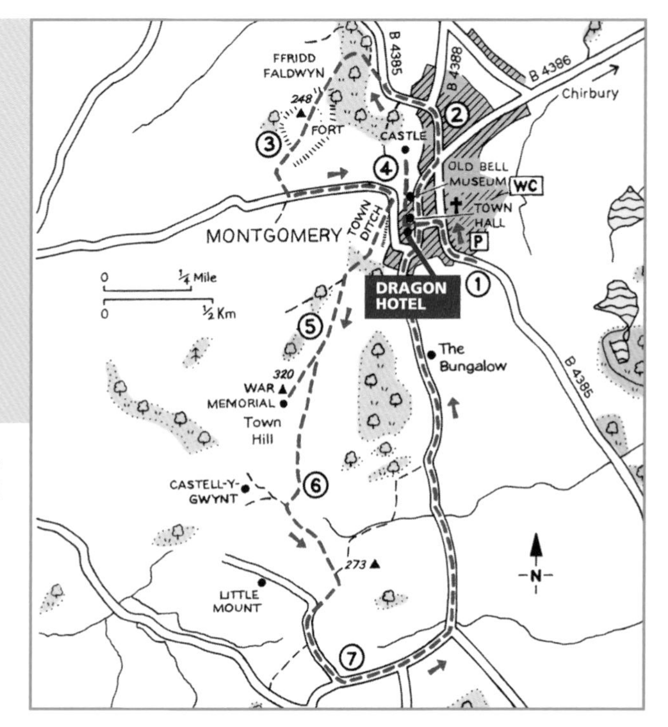

21: Linking the castles of Montgomery

Montgomery is a fine country town with its origins in medieval times, tucked beneath a castle-topped crag.

The centrepieces of Montogomery are the elegant red-brick town hall with a clock tower on top, and the half-timbered **Dragon Hotel**. Plaques on the walls of the old houses tell you of Montgomery's proud history, but you can learn more by calling into the Old Bell Inn, which has been converted into a museum.

After William I conquered England in 1066 he gave the task of controlling the Welsh Marches to his friend and staunch supporter, Roger de Montgomery. Montgomery set up a motte-and-bailey castle at Hendomen a mile (1.6km) north of the present town. There were continuous skirmishes with the Welsh, especially with the coming to power of Llewelyn the Great, Prince of Wales. As a result, Henry III had the current castle built in 1223 on a huge rock overlooking the plains of the River Severn.

In 1541 the new English monarch, Henry VII, a Welshman descended from Llewelyn, handed the castle to the powerful Herbert family. The castle saw its last action during the Civil War. The Royalist Herberts at first held the castle, but in a battle in which their 5,000 troops were attacked by 3,000 Parliamentarians, it was the Parliamentarians who were finally victorious. In 1649 they demolished the castle, but it's still an impressive place.

The next castle you see on the walk is much earlier. As you emerge from the woods, the sight of the giant earthworks of Ffridd Faldwyn makes it obvious that this hilltop Iron-Age fort was of great importance. It was built in four stages, all completed before the Roman conquest. Archaeological artefacts from the site, including neolithic tools, are now held in the National Museum of Wales in Cardiff.

Walk directions

❶ From the car park head north, then left along Broad Street, where you'll see the **Dragon Hotel** and the town hall. A signpost points to the lane up to the castle – a must to see, and it's free. Return to this point. Head north up Arthur Street, past the Old Bell Museum, and join the main road, Princes Street.

❷ Continue north, ignoring the turn for Chirbury, then turn left out of town along Station Road, the B4385. Ignore the first footpath on the left side of the road, but go over the stile and cross the field at the second stile. This path climbs through woodland, then swings left (south-west) to reach the old hilltop fort above Ffridd Faldwyn.

❸ Go over the stile at the far side of the fort and descend across more fields to the roadside gate. Turn left down the road, which takes you back towards Montgomery.

❹ As the road turns sharp right just above the town, leave it for a footpath on the right signposted to the Montgomeryshire War Memorial and beginning beyond a kissing gate. The footpath climbs steadily up the hill to join a farm track, which runs parallel to the 13th-century defensive town ditch at first.

❺ As it enters high pastures, the track begins to level out and traverse the eastern hillside. Here you can make a detour to the war memorial that lies clearly ahead at the top of the hill. Return to the track and follow it through a gate and past some pens with gorse and hawthorn lining the way on the left.

❻ In a field above Castell-y-gwynt farm, on the left-hand side, the footpath turns right to follow a hedge. Go over the stile at the far side of the field and turn left along a farm lane that descends to join a narrow tarmac country lane south-west of Little Mount farm. Turn left along this.

❼ Turn left at the first T-junction and left at the second. Follow the lane back into Montgomery to return to the welcoming **Dragon.**

Dragon Hotel

Montgomery SY15 6PA
Tel: 01686 668359
Directions: *A483 toward Welshpool, then right onto the B4385; the hotel is behind the town hall*
Open: *11–11*
Bar meals: *lunch and dinner served all week, 12–2, 7–9*
Restaurant: *lunch and dinner by booking only, 12–2, 7–9; average 3 course £19.50–£25*
Brewery/company: *free house*
Principle beers: *Wood Special, Interbrew Bass*
Children welcome
Parking: *20*
Rooms: *20 bedrooms en suite*

With its striking *black-and-white timbered frontage and historic interior, there is much to please the eye at this friendly, family-run coaching inn, parts of which date from the mid-17th century. Beams in the bar, lounge and some bedrooms are believed to have come from the destroyed castle.*

The best available local beef, lamb and fresh fish are featured in the regular menu and daily specials. Bar snacks include baked potatoes and jumbo Welsh rarebit specials, and freshly cooked main courses include steak, chicken Havana grilled with a spicy Cuban marinade, paella (for a minimum of two people), and rich pork sausages with mash. Food can be served in the garden.

The hotel offers overnight guests a wide range of facilities, including an indoor swimming pool and sauna.

Walk information

Distance: 5 miles (8km) + extension 2¾ miles (4.4km)
Map: OS Outdoor Leisure 45 The Cotswolds
Start/finish: Chipping Campden High Street or main square; grid ref SP 154393
Ascent/gradient: 2
Paths: Fields, roads and tracks; 8 stiles
Landscape: Open hillside, woodland and village

Rooftops of Chipping Campden

Look for

On reaching Dover's Hill, the route almost doubles back on itself – this is necessary in order to observe legal rights of way. Spend a little time poring over the topograph – on a clear day there is much to try to identify. In Campden, look out for the 14th-century Grevel's House, opposite Church Lane. William Grevel, called 'the flower of the wool merchants of all England', is thought to have been the inspiration for the merchant in William Chaucer's *The Canterbury Tales*.

22: Tracking down the Cotswold Olimpicks

Nowadays, these games are a cross between pantomime and carnival, but have retained their atmosphere of local fun.

The Cotswold Olimpicks bear only a passing resemblance to their more famous international counterpart. Established with the permission of James I, they were dubbed 'royal' games, and indeed have taken place during the reign of 14 monarchs. What they lack in grandeur and razzmatazz, however, they make up for in picturesqueness and local passion. Far from being a multi-million dollar shrine to technology, the stadium is a natural amphitheatre – the summit of Dover's Hill, on the edge of the Cotswold escarpment. The hill, with spectacular views westwards over the Vale of Evesham, is an English version of the site of the Greek original.

Dover's Hill is named after the founder of the Cotswold Olimpicks, Robert Dover, born in Norfolk in 1582. It is generally accepted that the first games took place in 1612, but they may well have begun at an earlier date. It is also possible that Dover was simply reviving an existing ancient festivity. Initially, at least, the main events were horse-racing and hare-coursing, the prizes being a silver castle ornament and a silver-studded collar. Other competitions in these early games were for running, jumping, throwing, wrestling and staff fighting. The area was festooned with yellow flags and ribbons, and there were dancing events as well as pavilions for chess and other similarly cerebral contests.

The Olimpicks soon became an indispensable part of the local Whitsuntide festivities, with mention of them even being made in Shakespeare's work. Dover managed the games for 30 years, and died in 1652. The games continued in various forms throughout the following centuries, surviving attempts to suppress them when they became more rowdy, and finally becoming an established annual event once again in 1966. Today they culminate torchlit procession back down to Chipping Campden.

Walk directions

❶ Turn left from the **Eight Bells** (Point Ⓐ on the extension loop), continue to the Catholic church, and turn right into West End Terrace. Where this bears right, go straight ahead on Hoo Lane. Follow this up to a right turn, with farm buildings on your left. Continue uphill over a stile to a path and keep going to a road.

❷ Turn left for a few paces and then right to cross to a path. Follow this along the field edge to a stile. Go over to Dover's Hill and follow the hedge to a stile with extensive views before you. Turn left along the escarpment edge, which drops away to your right. Pass a trig point and then a topograph. Now go right, down the slope, to a kissing gate on the left. Go through to a road and turn right.

❸ After 150 yards (137m) turn left over a stile into a field. Cross this and find a gate in the bottom right-hand corner. Head straight down the next field. At a stile go into another field and, keeping to the left of a fence, continue to another stile. Head down the next field, cross a track and then find adjacent stiles in the bottom left corner.

❹ Cross the first one and walk along the bottom of a field. Keep the stream and fence to your right and look for a stile in the far corner. Go over, crossing the stream, and then turn left, following a rising woodland path alongside the stream. Enter a field through a gate and continue ahead to meet a track. Stay on this, passing through gateposts, until you come to a country lane and turn left.

❺ After 400 yards (366m) reach a busier road and turn left for a further 450 yards (411m). Shortly before the road curves left, drop to the right on to a field path parallel

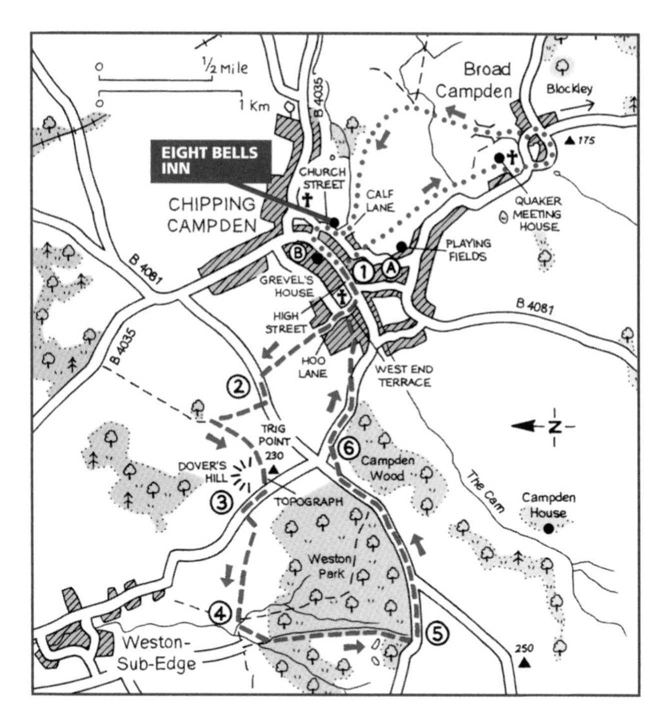

with the road. About 200 yards (183m) before the next corner go half right down the field to a road.

❻ Turn right, down the road. Shortly after a cottage on the right, go left into a field. Turn right over a stile and go half left to the corner. Pass through a kissing gate, cross a road among houses and continue ahead to meet West End Terrace. Turn right to return to the centre of Chipping Campden and the **Eight Bells** pub.

Extension to Broad Campden

Chipping Campden's near neighbour, Broad Campden, has some exceptionally pretty houses (several of which are thatched), an attractive pub and a 17th-century Quaker's Meeting House, all in a snug, overlooked fold of the Cotswold countryside.

From the High Street, walk through the arch next to the Noel Arms Hotel (Point Ⓐ) and continue ahead to join a path. Pass playing fields to reach a junction with a road. Go left here, into a field, then immediately right, to follow the field edge parallel with the road. After 600 yards (549m) fork right to a gate. Enter a drive, walk past a house and then leave the drive to walk ahead to a gate. Pass through into an alley and follow it to pass the Quakers' Meeting House.

Emerge at the green, with the church to your left. At a junction continue ahead to walk through the village. The road bears left and straightens. After the turning for

Eight Bells Inn

Church St, Chipping Campden
GL55 6JG
Tel: 01386 840371
Open: *11.30–3, 5.30–11*
(Jul–Aug 11–11)
Bar meals: *lunch and dinner served all week, 12–2.30, 6.30–9.30; average main course £10*
Restaurant: *lunch and dinner served all week, 12–2.30, 6.30–9.30*
Brewery/company: *free house*
Principal beers: *Hook Norton Best, Goff's Jouster*
Children welcome
Dogs allowed

A tiny, low *Cotswold stone frontage conceals two atmospheric, cosy bars where both good ales and good food are taken seriously. It was built in the 14th century to house the stonemasons and store the bells during construction of the nearby church, and the original oak beams, open fireplaces and even a priest's hole still survive. The pub continues to play a role as a supplier of refreshment to this historic wool and silversmith town, although many customers are now tourists. During the summer it is hung with attractive flower baskets. The pub can be entered through a cobbled entranceway; two bars lead through to the dining room and an enclosed courtyard for drinking and dining. Terraced gardens overlook the almshouses and the church.*

In these unspoilt surroundings, freshly prepared local food is offered on a daily changing menu. Options range from salads and lighter dishes to full Sunday lunch. You might start your meal with a twice-baked cheese soufflé served with salad, or a warm salad of lambs' kidneys with black pudding and toasted pine kernels. Robust main courses include Mr Lashford's pork, leek and apple sausages with creamed mash and onion gravy, or slowly braised lamb kleftiko set on a sweet potato purée. For a fishy alternative try seared fillets of brill on a tomato and red onion compôte and drizzled with crab bisque, or whole lemon sole with a lemon, caper and cherry tomato butter sauce. Food theme nights include Indian, Thai and Mexican fare.

Blockley, go left down a road marked 'Unsuitable for Motors'. After 70 yards (64m) turn right along the drive of 'Hollybush'. Pass through a gate and then another to continue along the left, lower margin of an orchard.

Cross a stile, then a bridge and turn sharp right along the right-hand field edge, with the stream on your right. Cross the stream at the end of the field and, in the next field, go straight across, bearing right to a gap. Go up the next field to a stile and cross into a field. Turn left and then go half-right to pass to the right of a house.

Cross a stile, then go half-right to a gate. Go through and bear right, down to another stile in the corner. In the next field go half-right, with Chipping Campden church away to the right, to approach a stream near a stone arch. Do not cross the stream but, 70 yards (64m) after the arch, turn right through a gate and follow the path as it turns left to a drive. Turn right and follow the drive to Calf Lane. Turn right and, at the top, turn left into Church Street (Point **B**) to return to a junction with the main street (or right to visit the magnificent church). Turn left to return to the start.

23: A walk to mellow Chastleton and beyond

'isit Chastleton House, a splendid Jacobean mansion owned by he National Trust, on this lovely walk to the village of Adlestrop.

he village was immortalised by ne Edwardian poet Edward homas in his 1915 poem, 'Yes, I emember Adlestrop', about eing marooned on a sleepy ailway when the train stopped.

Valk directions

From the attractive old **Fox** ub turn right and walk through ne village to a left turning pposite Forge House. Follow the ane to the church of St Nicholas. eep it on your left, avoid a left- and footpath and take the next eft bridleway. Head down hrough fields, following vaymarks, and turn right in the ottom corner to reach a ootbridge.

❷ Cross over to a gate and follow the track ahead over the railway line. Keep ahead alongside a hedge and turn right at the road. Pass New Farm and turn left at the next bridleway sign. Head down towards Daylesford House, keep left at the fork and follow the drive between paddocks.

❸ Pass the estate office and turn left by Hill Farm Cottage. Pass between buildings, cross over at an intersection of tracks and break cover from the trees. Swing right after several hundred yards and follow waymarks, cutting diagonally right across a paddock to a gate in the corner. Continue ahead, through trees, to the A436.

❹ Turn left, pass a turning to Adlestrop and turn right at the stile. Follow the woodland path to a track. Turn right to the road and cross over to Long Drive. Follow it to some gates and turn right. Skirt a field, keeping woodland on the right, and continue ahead between fields to reach the road on a bend. Keep ahead to Chastleton House.

❺ Turn left beyond the bend and pass through an avenue of trees to join the Macmillan Way long distance path. Descend through fields and follow the path to a track. Keep ahead to the road and cross over to Adlestrop's preserved railway sign. Keep it on your left and walk through the village, veering right for the church.

❻ Join a track beyond it and make for a lake and kissing gate. Keep to the left of the cricket ground, pass between four trees and follow the sunken path to two stiles leading to the road. Turn left to the A436, turn right and then take the turning to Lower Oddington. Return to the welcoming **Fox.**

Valk information

)istance: 7 miles (11.3km)
Aap: OS Outdoor Leisure 45 The .otswolds
tart/finish: Fox, Lower)ddington; grid ref SP 232259
.scent/gradient: 2
'aths: country roads, bridleways, ield and woodland paths, drives nd tracks; 2 stiles
andscape: rolling Cotswold andscape

he Jacobean mansion of Chastleton

Fox

Lower Oddington GL56 0UR
Tel: 01451 870555
Directions: *take the A436 from Stow-on-the-Wold, then go right to Lower Oddington*
Open: *12–11*
Bar meals: *lunch and dinner served all week, 12–2.30, 6.30–10*
Restaurant: *lunch and dinner served all week, 12–2.30, 6.30–10*
Brewery/company: *free house*
Principal beers: *Hook Norton Best, Badger Tanglefoot, Abbot Ale, Tag Ruddles, County*
Children welcome
Parking: *14*
Rooms: *d£58*

Under the still relatively new *ownership of James Cathcart and Ian Mackenzie, the Fox benefits from one of the most idyllic and unspoilt village locations in the Cotswolds. Its 16th-century, mellow stone façade is largely hidden by dense Virginia creeper, while inside you'll be greeted by polished slate floors, fresh flowers and candles on pine tables, tasteful prints on rag-washed walls, a blazing log fire in the convivial bar and daily papers.*

You'll find a rare commitment to all things good here – food, wine, real ale, accommodation and company – the Fox is very successful at enticing visitors away from the honeypots of Stow-on-the-Wold, Moreton-in-Marsh and Chipping Norton. And why shouldn't it be? It serves well kept beers, fine wines, good imaginative food, and offers warm efficient and friendly service. The menu takes full advantage of the seasons and changes regularly.

Starters might include rough and smooth patés with apple and fig chutney, and courgette and stilton risotto. Coq au vin is always in demand, and fresh Scottish salmon baked in filo pastry with wild mushroom and chive sauce, and grilled organic sausages with celeriac and potato puree and Cumberland sauce are also popular. Other fresh fish comes up from Cornwall and features on the regular menu – baked sea trout with creamed leeks and saffron, for example – and the daily specials board. For pudding try the delicious dark chocolate torte, or blueberry crème brûlée.

Booking is recommended for rare roast beef and Yorkshire pudding on Sundays. The pub has an awning-covered, heated terrace and a pretty, traditional cottage garden

Accommodation is in three tastefully decorated bedrooms.

24: An Oxfordshire mystery revealed

A stone fireplace set in a bank in an Oxfordshire churchyard is virtually all that is left of Cumnor Place, the setting for a mystery that has baffled historians for centuries.

The manor of Cumnor was once owned by Abingdon Abbey and the remains of the house, the abbot's summer residence, form part of the extended parish churchyard. Cumnor Place, which stood to the west of the church, was demolished in 1810. Its remains are a reminder of a scandal which briefly rocked Elizabethan England.

The house was leased by Anthony Forster, steward to Robert Dudley, Elizabeth I's favourite. Dudley married Amy Robsart in 1550. She was the only daughter of a wealthy Norfolk landowner, and only 18 when she married, but the couple seemed happy together – at least on the face of it.

Three years later Dudley found himself in the Tower of London, charged with conspiring against Mary Tudor. He was later pardoned, but the death of Mary in 1558 and the accession of Elizabeth to the throne had a significant impact on Dudley. He and the new Queen had been friends since childhood and now they would become even closer. Elizabeth was certainly smitten – it is said she smiled on no-one as she smiled on Dudley.

While Dudley spent much of his time court, Amy stayed with friends in the country. She was lonely, and there were rumours that she was ailing. In 1560 she went to stay with Anthony Forster and his wife at Cumnor Place. On Sunday 8 September, Amy died after apparently falling downstairs and breaking her neck.

On hearing the news at court, Dudley allegedly showed no outward signs of grief or distress, perhaps fearing that the circumstances surrounding his wife's death would damage his reputation. But what had really killed his young wife? Was it suicide, natural causes, a tragic accident or, worst of all, murder? If so, was Forster involved? Forster knew that if Dudley were free to marry the Queen, then his own future would be assured.

Nothing about Amy's mysterious death has ever been proved. A jury at the time returned a verdict of 'mischance or accidental death'. The Queen didn't marry Dudley, but within three years of Amy's death she promoted him to the powerful role of Earl of Leicester.

Walk information

Distance: 6 miles (9.7km) + extension 1 mile (1.6km)
Map: OS Explorer 180 Oxford
Start/finish: parking spaces by village hall, Cumnor; grid ref SP 458044
Ascent/gradient: negligible
Paths: field paths, quiet lanes and tracks; 1 stile
Landscape: fields and pasture beside the River Thames

Walk directions

❶ Turn right from the parking area and walk along to the mini-roundabout. Turn right into Appleton Road and pass the **Bear and Ragged Staff** pub on the right. Veer half-left just a few paces beyond it and join a footpath signposted to Bessels Leigh. Pass the cricket club on the left and continue on the track. When it peters out continue ahead in the field, keeping a ditch on your right. Pass along a line of trees on the far side of the field, turn left, then turn right and make for an opening in the corner (may be concealed by vegetation in summer). Go straight on to a galvanised gate and keep some houses over to the left, beyond the pasture. Cross a footbridge to a galvanised gate, swing left and cross the field towards the road. Keep in line with telephone wires and make for a waymark in the

While there

Pause and savour the peace and tranquillity of Bablock Hythe. The 19th-century poet Matthew Arnold knew this place well and made references to Bablock Hythe and the surrounding countryside in his work. It was his 'Scholar Gipsy' who 'oft was met crossing the stripling Thames at Bablock-hythe.' The Romans crossed the river here, and a ferry has operated for more than 1,000 years.

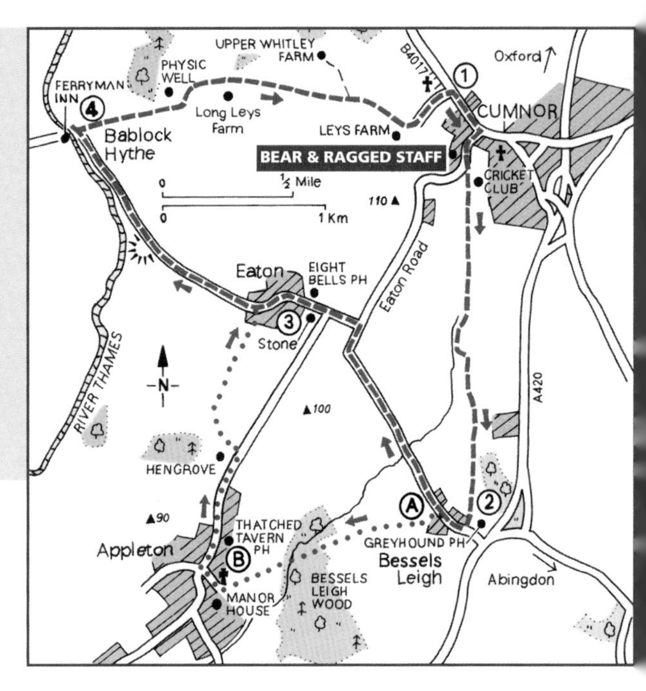

field corner. Follow the drive to the road.

2 Turn right (the start of the Appleton extension is soon to your left) and follow the road through Bessels Leigh and continue out in the countryside, cutting between farmland. On reaching a junction, keep left to the next junction. Go straight on into the village of Eaton and pass the Eight Bells pub.

3 Follow the lane out of Eaton and through flat countryside. When it becomes enclosed by trees, look for a view of the Thames on the left. Continue to Bablock Hythe and look across the river to the Ferryman Inn. Walk back along the lane for a few paces and turn left at the bridleway signposted 'Cumnor'.

4 Pass through a gate and when, some time later, the path curves to the left, look for the Physic Well in the trees to the left of your route. This is a muddy spring which was once greatly valued as a source of healing waters. Emerge from the trees and cut between fields towards pylons. Go through a gate, join a drive and walk ahead. Ignore the turning to Upper Whitley Farm and continue into Cumnor, passing Leys Farm on the right. Look for the United Reformed church and return to the village hall and the **Bear and Ragged Staff.**

Extension to Appleton

Appleton is a picturesque village of brick and stone houses. The manor house is partly 12th-century, and its Norman doorway is visible over the churchyard wall. Inside the Norman church is a tomb to a member of the Fettiplace family, who was knighted by Elizabeth I when she visited Woodstock.

Turn left at the sign for Appleton and go through the galvanised gate, Point **A**. Follow the track/road to the right and straight along to two sets of galvanised gates and some farm outbuildings on the right. Continue across the pasture to a kissing gate leading into Bessels

Look for

As you enter Eaton by road from Bessels Leigh, look for a memorial stone by the entrance to West Farm. The stone recalls that the trees here were given by staff and friends of A Howard Cornish MBE JP (1895–1964), County Alderman and lifelong farmer here.

Bear and Ragged Staff

28 Appleton Rd, Cumnor
OX2 9QH
Tel: 01865 862329
Directions: *take the A20 from Oxford, turn right to Cumnor on B4017*
Open: *12–11 (Sun 12–10.30)*
Bar meals: *lunch and dinner served all week, 12–3, 6–9.30; average main course £11.50*
Restaurant: *lunch and dinner served all week, 12–3, 6–10; average 3 course à la carte £20*
Brewery/company: *Morrells*
Principal beers: *Morrells IPA, Old Speckled Hen, Abbot Ale, Old Hooky*
Children welcome
Dogs allowed
Parking: *60*

The Bear and *Ragged Staff, which is the emblem for the Earls of Warwick and the county emblem for Warwickshire, lies on the edge of Cumnor. It's a 700-year-old pub dating back to Cromwell's days, and allegedly haunted by the mistress of the Earl of Warwick. Cromwell's brother Richard is believed to have chiselled out the royal crest from above one of the fireplaces. The wooden interior, including two original massive fireplaces, adds to the atmosphere, and the appeal is enhanced by soft furnishings and warm colours.*

The pub caters for a wide cross-section of locals as well as being a popular destination for lovers of good food. Freshly prepared meals with full service might produce starters like smoked duck breast on a mixed leaf salad, or timbale of salmon, crab and prawns, followed by monkfish in smoked bacon with saffron sauce, or Thai chicken curry, and perhaps profiteroles with Chantilly cream and a rich chocolate sauce. A good range of Havana cigars, ports and brandies.

Leigh Wood. This area has been continuously wooded for over 400 years. Roe, fallow and muntjac deer are known to inhabit the woods.

Pass a stile and footpath on the right and continue ahead through the wood. Emerging from the trees, cut across a footbridge and follow a straight path between fences and pastures. Cross a stile and footbridge and approach Appleton church. Pass to the side of it to the drive and follow it into the village. Follow Church Road to the T-junction and turn right opposite the post office and stores, Point **B**.

Walk along to the Thatched Tavern and then head out of Appleton, passing the village sign. Just a few paces beyond the entrance to a house called Hengrove, turn left at a footpath sign for Eaton. Follow the track as it sweeps to the right and skirts the field, keeping alongside the boundary. Join a clear track on a bend and continue ahead. Pass some farm outbuildings to reach the road at Eaton, rejoining the main walk at this point.

25: Where the Maharajah made his mark

Enclosed by an exotic cupola, the Maharajah's Well might be a familiar landmark in Stoke Row but first-time visitors gaze curiously at this spectacle, unsure if they can believe their eyes.

Walk information

Distance: 5 miles (8km)
Map: OS Explorer 171 Chiltern Hills West
Start/finish: roadside parking in Stoke Row; grid ref SU 678840
Ascent/gradient: 1
Paths: field and woodland paths and tracks, road (busy); 8 stiles
Landscape: Chiltern woodland and farmland

The well was given to the village by the Maharajah of Benares in 1863 as a gift.

The story goes that the Indian ruler met Edward Anderdon Reade (soon to become Lieutenant-Governor of the North West Provinces of India) in Benares. The Maharajah indicated his plans to overcome the acute local water shortage, and Anderdon Reade agreed that it was a familiar problem at home in the Chilterns. In villages like Stoke Row, he explained, locals relied on rainwater for their cooking, and so precious was it that it was often passed from one cooking pot to the next.

During the Indian Mutiny, Anderdon Reade was able to help the Maharajah of Benares. To express his gratitude, and as a token of friendship, the Maharajah decided to presented Stoke Row with the gift of a well, with the condition 'that the public should have the privilege of taking water free of charge in all time to come.'

The well was officially opened on 24 May 1864 – Queen Victoria's birthday. The beneficent Maharajah in later years made other gifts to the village, including a new footpath to the well. In 1906 mains water was piped to Stoke Row, but the well was still in use until 1939.

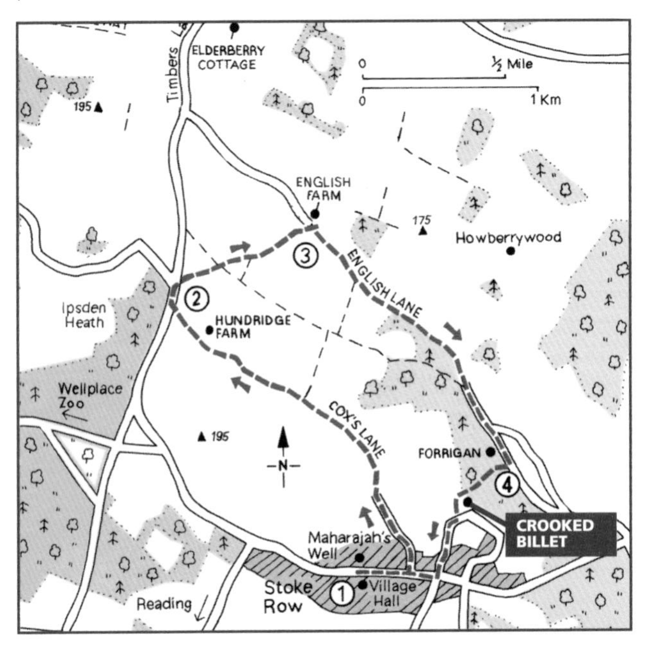

Walk directions

❶ From the car park turn right and walk past the village stores. Turn left into Cox's Lane and follow it as it curves to the left. Soon it dwindles to a track. Continue to a waymark, avoid the footpath on the right and keep ahead on the right of way. The track narrows to a path now, running between trees and hedgerows. Pass a stile and footpath and eventually you reach the outbuildings of Hundridge Farm. Join a track running through the woodland and make for the road.

❷ Turn right along the road for

Look for

Together with the adjoining well, the Cherry Orchard was given to the village by the Maharajah of Benares. One hundred and one cherry trees were originally planted to provide an income to help fund the upkeep of the well. Today the orchard is a village open space, its upkeep dependent on local support.

Crooked Billet

Stoke Row RG9 5PU
Tel: 01491 681048
Directions: *from the A4130 Henley–Oxford, turn left at Nettlebed for Stoke Row*
Open: *12–11 (Sun 12–10.30)*
Bar meals: *lunch and dinner served all week 12–2.30, 7–10; average cost of main course £12.95*
Restaurant: *lunch and dinner served all week, 12–2.30, 7–10*
Brewery/company: *Brakspear*
Principal beers: *Brakspear Bitter*
Children welcome
Parking: *50*

A rustic country *gastro-pub hidden away down a single-track lane in deepest Oxfordshire, the Crooked Billet has a casual, informal atmosphere and friendly service. It was built in 1642, and was once the hideout of the notorious highwayman Dick Turpin, who courted the landlord's daughter. Today it retains all the original old-world charm of the true country pub. It is delightfully unspoilt inside with low beams, ancient tiled floors, open fires and simple furnishings. Famed for its food, it attracts local celebrities, including several introduced by the late George Harrison. Kate Winslett held her wedding reception here, and it continues to draw the well heeled and the well known.*

Local produce and organic fare are the mainstay of the kitchen. Expect sautéed partridge and wild mushroom fricasée, pan-fried bass with baby squid, roast Mediterranean vegetables and salsa verde, and pink-carved venison with haggis, baby spinach, roast figs and a port,redcurrant and juniper sauce. Grilled turbot with buttered spinach, seared scallops and prawn, champagne and chive sauce is one of the seafood specials, along with sea bream tagliatelle with confit of tomatoes, olives and gremolina. A separate vegetarian choice lists the likes of Moroccan vegetable tagine with Marrakech mint and coriander couscous and spicy harissa dipping pot. Puddings include Bakewell tart with custard sauce, and champagne and fresh raspberry trifle.

several paces, then swing right at the footpath sign into the wood. Follow the path between trees and cross a drive. Make for a stile ahead and then go diagonally right in the field, using the waymark posts to guide you. Look for a stile in the corner and cross a lane to a further stile on the opposite side. Head diagonally right in the field and look for a stile by a hard tennis court. Pass alongside a beech hedge to a drive and turn left. As the drive sweeps left to a house, go forward over a cattle grid to a field. Continue with the boundary on your left and on reaching the corner, go straight on along a track.

3 Turn right at English Farm and follow the narrow track known as English Lane. Pass a footpath and stile on the right-hand side and follow the track along the edge of woodland. Continue to a junction and keep ahead through the trees. Pass a timber-framed cottage on the left-hand side and a house on the right called Forrigan. Keep ahead for about 100 yards (91m) and swing right at a sign for Stoke Row.

4 Cross a stile and cut through the wood to a second stile. Emerge from the woodland at a gate and cross a pasture to a further patch of woodland. Negotiate the next stile within sight of the **Crooked Billet** pub and go up a gentle slope towards the pub. Turn right at the road, pass a footpath on the right, followed by Rose Cottage, and head for the crossroads in the centre of Stoke Row. Turn right and return to the start of the walk.

Walk information

Distance: 5½miles (8.8 km)
Map: OS Explorer 245 The National Forest
Start/finish: Ye Olde Dog & Partridge Inn, Tutbury; grid ref SK 214289
Ascent/gradient: 2
Paths: paths and tracks, lots of stiles
Landscape: undulating country on the Staffordshire/Derbyshire border, to the south of the River Dove

The ruins of Tutbury Castle

26: Wartime memories at Tutbury

The walk passes romantic castle ruins, pretty farmland and Fauld Crater – a serious dent in the ground formed in 1944 when 4,000 tons of bombs stored in old gypsum mines exploded.

Walk directions

❶ From the timbered **Ye Olde Dog & Partridge Inn** turn left, then right at the mini-roundabout. Head towards the remains of the castle, passing the small museum and the Leopard pub. The road climbs the hill, bending left. A fingerpost marks a footpath between houses: follow this path down to a little gate by Tutbury Castle. Go straight on to the corner of the field, through a gateway and cross a stile immediately on your left, followed by a bridge.

❷ Turn right towards a footbridge in the hedge. Cross this and turn left, looking for a stile and fingerpost in the hedge. Walk over a large field, keeping straight on when the river winds away to the right. Cross a stile by a hedge corner and go straight ahead in the field to the next stile. Keep ahead to meet the road at Boundary House.

❸ Turn right along the road and then left at the fingerpost by the Fauld Industrial Estate. Follow the estate road to a stile to the right of some large gates. Descend the bank and go straight on, with the hedge on your right. Cross the next stile and turn left up a track. Beyond the next stile bend slightly right to follow the path with woodland on the left. Cross a stile, turn right to go uphill. Keep the wire fence well to your left and cross a stile to enter the wood.

❹ Pass a pheasant enclosure on your left, and at an area of open ground go right into the trees, then left at a grain hopper. Keep left when the track bends right and climb a steep slope. Go through a kissing gate at the top to reach the crater. Seventy people died in the accident, and an entire farm was destroyed.

❺ Keep walking straight ahead,

'e Olde Dog & 'artridge Inn

'igh St, Tutbury, nr Burton upon ent DE13 9LS
l: 01283 813030
'rections: on A50 north-west Burton upon Trent (signed from e A50 and the A511)
pen: 11.45–2, 6–11
estaurant: lunch served Tue–Sun, 45–2; dinner served Tue–Sat, –9.45; average 3 course £19.95
ewery/company: free house
'incipal beers: Marston's Pedigree
hildren welcome
rking: 100
ooms: 20 bedrooms en suite om s£75, d£69

ass a footpath on the right, and ntinue along the hedgerow to here another path joins from e right. Turn sharp left and cross e field to a stile. Keep the hedge 1 your right, crossing the aymarked stiles past Hare Holes rm and up to Castle Hayes rm. Bend slightly left here, past e farm, avoiding two tracks on e left.

At an arrow pointing left, llow the track to a stile and keep ong a hedge to a stile on the ght. Veer left and follow the path ound to the right. Turn left at e bottom of a slope and follow e path to the road at Owen's ank. Cross over to the stile and ead diagonally across the field, ith the castle ahead. Rejoin the ath, turn left and return to the **Ye lde Dog & Partridge Inn.**

The inn has *stood here since the 15th century. A beautiful period building in a charming village, resplendent in its timbers and whitewashed walls, with abundant flower displays beneath the windows. when Henry IV was on the throne. Its connection with the village sport of bull-running brought it into prominence, and it remains a focus of local activity including the nearby hunt. During the 18th century it became a coaching inn on the route to London. Five hundred years of offering hospitality has resulted in a well deserved reputation for good food, comfortable accommodation and restful public areas. Bedrooms, which include four-posters and half-testers, are individually furnished and filled with modern luxuries.*

Two smart eating outlets ensure that all tastes are catered for. In the Carvery, a grand piano plays while diners choose from an extensive menu; start with a selection from the buffet, or go for fisherman's platter, or woodman's mushrooms, and follow on with a plate of roast meat, or perhaps tasty steak and kidney pie, or ratatouille bake.

In the brasserie, with its leather chairs and bare wooden tables, the fixed price menu may list fallen Dovedale blue cheese soufflé, or terrine of tame and wild duck, followed by chargrilled swordfish loin with mango and chilli salsa, or breast of guinea fowl. Make sure you leave time and space for mouth-watering desserts like chocolate truffle torte, and pear and almond tart.

27: Discovering the delights of Warwick

This easy walk offers the opportunity to visit one of the most famous castles in England.

Starting from the car park at Warwick Racecourse, a stroll along the towpath of the Grand Union Canal to the River Avon brings you to Castle Bridge. This is always considered to give the classic view of Warwick's magnificent castle.

Walk information

Distance: 5 miles (8km) + extension 2¼ miles (3.6km)
Map: OS Explorer 221 Coventry & Warwick
Start/finish: Warwick Racecourse car park; grid ref SP 277647
Ascent/gradient: 1
Paths: canal and riverside paths, street pavements; 2 stiles
Landscape: canalside and historic town

Dating from the 14th century, Warwick Castle sits imperiously above the River Avon near the centre of the town. It is the ancestral home of the Earls of Warwick, of which Richard Beauchamp (1428–71) is the most famous. He lived through the reign of three kings and was present at the burning of Joan of Arc. In 1461 he replaced Henry VI with Edward, Duke of York and made himself virtual ruler of England until 1464. When, in 1470, he fell out with Edward, he fled to France and formed an alliance with Margaret of Anjou, wife of the deposed Henry VI. Warwick promptly invaded England, defeated Edward IV and restored Henry VI to the throne. For this feat he became known as 'Warwick the Kingmaker'.

You can spend a whole day at Warwick Castle, there is so much to see. Inside you can admire the tapestry of the gardens of Versailles, Oliver Cromwell's helmet, Queen Anne's travelling trunk and Marie Antoinette's clock. Outside, wonderful gardens laid out by Lancelot 'Capability' Brown in the 18th century beckon. The 'Warwick Vase', discovered in the grounds of Hadrian's villa at Trivoli, can be found in a greenhouse in the garden.

Tear yourself away from the castle to continue the walk, through the county town of 'Shakespeare Country'. It displays a fascinating blend of Georgian and Tudor architecture. In Castle Street you pass the timbered home of Thomas Oken – now housing a doll museum. St Mary's Church is up the road opposite. You can climb its great 174-foot (53-m)

Warwick Castle, from the bridge

While there

No trip to Warwick is complete without a visit to fantastic Warwick Castle, but do walk carefully as you enter the eerie Ghost Tower for you may not be alone. It was here, in 1628, that the castle's then owner, Sir Fulke Greville, was fatally stabbed by a manservant because he did not bequeath sufficient funds to him in his will. Note that entry to the castle isn't cheap. It's open 10–6 April to September, and 10–5 October to March.

tower for a fantastic view of the town and the surrounding countryside. Inside the church is the 15th-century Beauchamp Chapel. The tomb of Ambrose Dudley, Earl of Leicester is said to have been made by the same craftspeople who modelled Shakespeare's bust at Stratford. The **Tilted Wig** is close by.

Before heading back to the racecourse you'll pass the magnificent medieval Lord Leycester's Hospital, at the West Gate of Warwick. This was originally the Guild House of St George which was transformed into the Almshouse in 1571 by Robert Dudley.

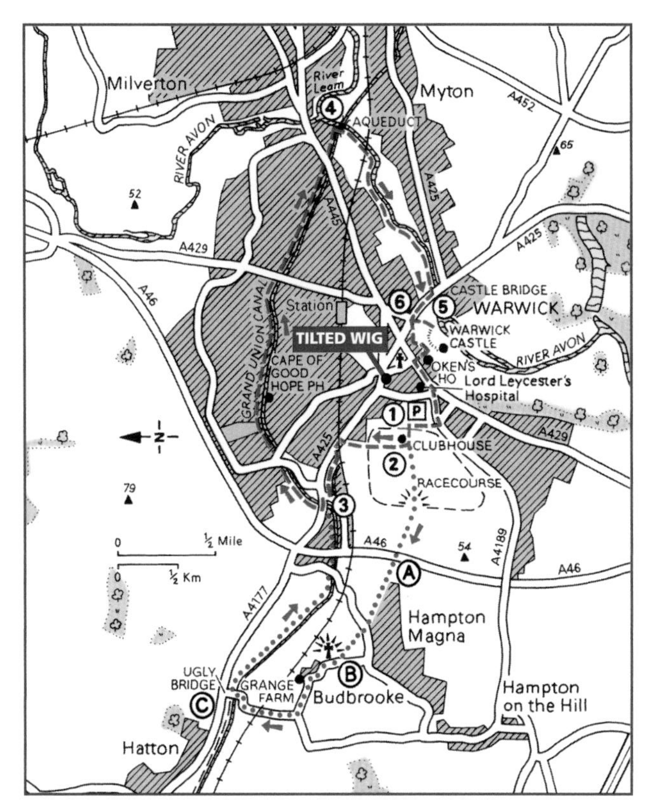

Walk directions

❶ Walk to the end of the racecourse car park and go left towards the golf clubhouse.

❷ (The extension walk starts from here.) Go right and take the wide green track between the golf course and the driving range. In about 300 yards (274m), cross over the racetrack and go over a stile on to a footpath by a small factory complex. Continue ahead and, at the corner of common land, go right over another stile onto a lane and descend to the road. Go left along the pavement beneath the railway bridge, then left again over a final stile onto grassland by the Saltisford Canal. Follow this grassy area to the towpath, passing a large narrowboat mooring area, and climb the steps up to the canal bridge and on to the pavement beside a road. Turn right along the pavement, and in 50 yards (46m) reach a bridge over the Grand Union Canal and the busy A425.

❸ Cross the road with care. Go left over the canal bridge and descend to take the towpath into Warwick, 1½ miles (2.4km) away, passing by a lock gate with the Cape of Good Hope pub opposite and then going along the back of residential properties. Shortly after passing by a Tesco store and just before reaching the aqueduct over the River Avon, go left down steps to join the 'Waterside Walk'.

❹ Proceed right under the aqueduct and follow the river bank footpath. At Castle Bridge, climb steps on to the pavement of the A425 (Banbury) road and cross with care.

Look for

As you walk up Castle Street you pass a very pretty timber-framed 15th-century house. This is Thomas Oken's House. Oken was a silk and luxury goods merchant who was a famous Warwick benefactor. He founded an almshouse for poor women, endowed a schoolmaster and provided money for bonfires for the young. Master of the Guild at the time of the 1545 town charter, he died, childless, in 1573.

Tilted Wig

11 Market Place, Warwick
CV34 4SA
Tel: 01926 410466
Directions: *from M40, junction 15, follow A429 into Warwick; after 1½ miles (2.4km) go left into Brook St and on into Market Place*
Open: *11–11 (Sun 12–10.30)*
Bar meals: *lunch served all week, 12–3; dinner served Mon–Sat, 6–9; average main course £7*

Brewery/company: *Punch Taverns*
Principal beers: *Carlsberg-Tetley Tetley Bitter, Adnams Broadside*
Children welcome
Parking: *6*
Rooms: *4 bedrooms en suite from s£58, d£58*

Overlooking the market *square of this historic county town, this attractive pine-furnished hostelry combines the atmosphere of a brasserie, wine bar and restaurant, all rolled into one. It was originally a coaching inn, and is now a Grade II listed building. The unusual name stems from its proximity to the Crown Court.*

A wide range of cask-conditioned ales is offered, and a good menu offers quality, home-cooked dishes, which might include cottage pie, tuna steak, whole-tailed scampi, Barnsley chop, chilli con carne, liver with bacon and onions, and tagliatelle.

❺ Stroll onto the bridge for the classic view of Warwick Castle, then turn around and follow the pavement towards Warwick town.

❻ In 220 yards (201m) go left and meander down picturesque Mill Street for the second classic view of the castle. Return to the main road and go left through the main entrance gate to Warwick Castle grounds. Bear right and leave the grounds via a wall gate into Castle Street. Stroll up Castle Street, passing Oken's House, until you reach the tourist information centre on the corner of the High Street. St Mary's Church is ahead if you wish to visit. Turn left here and walk along High Street, going beneath the archway of the Lord Leycester Hotel. Go right into Bowling Green Street and, in 50 yards (46m), turn left down Friars Street to reach Warwick Racecourse.

Extension to Ugly Bridge

From the golf driving range building (near Point ❷), continue ahead on the clearly waymarked footpath walking in a north-westerly direction. Before crossing the racetrack pause to enjoy a fine retrospective view over Warwick, then continue across pastureland, going over a couple of footbridges. When you reach the field hedge and the busy A46, cross it with care and follow the footpath to the left of the field hedge, climbing towards the village of Hampton Magna (Point Ⓐ).

The footpath takes you past a residential estate onto the Old Budbrooke Road, where a large stone recalls the history of the Warwickshire Regiment, whose barracks were once located here. Cross the road and continue over the stile opposite into meadow. The footpath arcs right, passing a pond, then veers left towards the church in the small village of Budbrooke (Point Ⓑ).

The 13th-century parish church is surrounded by lovely elm trees and contains a marble monument to Rowland Dormer. Grove Park, the home of the Dormers, an influential family, is located in wooded parkland near by. From the church there is a grand view of Warwick town, with the castle prominent amid the trees.

At the church car park, go right through the churchyard onto a lane. Go right again along the lane past Grange Farm and over the railway line to reach Ugly Bridge over the Grand Union Canal (Point Ⓒ).

Pause on the bridge and look north-west up the canal to see the flight of Hatton Lockgates. There are 21 locks and the canal rises some 140 feet (42m) over 2 miles (3.2km). You may be lucky enough to see a narrowboat making its way down the flight of locks. Now descend to the towpath and follow it, going south east towards Warwick. After passing six locks, including Hatton Bottom Lock (near Warwick Parkway railway station), rejoin the main walk by the A425 at Point ❸.

28: A coastal stroll at Brancaster Staithe

Walk information

Distance: 3½ miles (5.7km)
Map: OS Explorer 250 Norfolk Coast West
Start/finish: White Horse, Brancaster Staithe; grid ref TF 798444
Ascent/gradient: negligible
Paths: paths, tracks and roads
Landscape: open marshland, gorse and heather common

The coastal view from the White Horse

This spectacular walk follows the Norfolk Coast Path. Although widely remarked upon as 'Very flat, Norfolk', within the county boundaries lies a host of things to see and do.

Walking along the desolate and marshy coastline, one of the finest in Europe, offers a wonderful sense of space and freedom.

Walk directions

❶ Make for the bottom of the garden at the **White Horse** pub and turn right to join the Norfolk Coast Path. Walk for 500 yards (457m), enjoying the spectacular views to the wind-blown sand dunes of Scolt Head Island. Numerous species of bird swoop down in search of food as the tide comes in.

❷ Turn right to follow a lane known as the Drove (not signposted) towards Burnham Deepdale. Before crossing the A149 coast road, note 11th-century St Mary's Church. Its main claim to fame is a rare 11th-century font with figures representing the months of the year. Cross the road at the bus shelter, turn left into

White Horse

Main Rd, Brancaster Staithe, King's Lynn PE31 8BY
Tel: 01485 210262
Directions: *mid-way between King's Lynn and Wells-next-the-Sea on the A149 coastal road*
Open: *11.30–11 (Sun 12–10.30)*
Restaurant: *lunch and dinner served all week, 12–2, 7–9; average 3 course £22*
Brewery/company: *free house*
Principal beers: *Adnams Bitter, Regatta, Southwold & Fisherman, Greene King IPA*
Children welcome
Dogs allowed
Parking: *45*
Rooms: *15 bedrooms en suite*

Delgate Lane (not signposted) and walk south past Valley Farm on the right.

❸ Just beyond the farm you reach the Breaks, a woodland area that sailors out at sea once used as a navigation point. Continue for another few hundred yards and turn right at a lovely copse. Cut through it to a gated road on the right to Barrow Common. Gorse, ferns and a host of wild flowers bring this area to life.

❹ Take a path marked by a fingerpost about 20 feet (6m) to the left and follow it to where the old Branodunum fort, built to guard the approaches to the Wash, once stood. Retrace your steps to the road and turn towards the top of Barrow Common. Follow the road downhill, cross the A149 and turn left.

This gloriously located *and stylish dining pub is set beside the tidal marshes at Brancaster Staithe, with stunning views across the wildlife-rich coastline. Award-winning seafood can be enjoyed in the airy conservatory restaurant, the scrubbed bar or the summer sun deck. Scrubbed pine tables, high-backed settles, an open log fire in winter and cream painted walls contribute to the bright, welcoming atmosphere. In summer, the sun deck comes into its own, where diners can watch the small sailing boats heading for the harbour entrance, and the sea retreating from the salt marsh.*

With the sea so close, lovers of seafood and fish won't be disappointed, with mussels and crabs in season, cockle chowder, and Thai fishcakes on offer as both starter and main course. By no means, though, does the North Sea provide everything on the menu: daily blackboard specials may include Glamorgan sausages with tomato and basil sauce, lamb tagine and couscous and roasted celeriac, and mushroom and Parmesan tartlet, while salads, sandwiches and children's items are available too. The restaurant, overlooking a courtyard where the stagecoaches once arrived and departed, offers grilled breast of corn-fed chicken, and deep-fried spicy chickpea cake on cucumber and passion fruit raita. Home-made desserts include treacle tart and apple pie.

❺ Turn right shortly into Harbour Way. During the summer season you can catch a ferry from here to Scolt Head Island. Rejoin the Norfolk Coast Path in front of Brancaster Staithe Sailing Club and head east along the old quayside. Continue for about half a mile (800m) to the marsh-side entrance to the **White Horse.**

29: Exploring Lord Nelson's birthplace

In 1758 Edmund Nelson, rector of Burnham Thorpe, and his wife Catherine had their fifth child and named him Horatio, little dreaming that he would become a great naval hero.

The rectory where Horatio Nelson spent the first years of his life was later demolished, but when you extend the walk to Burnham Thorpe you'll see a plaque set in a wall where it once stood.

Nelson was just 12 when he entered the Royal Navy. He quickly gained experience, travelling as far afield as the Caribbean and the Arctic by the time he was 16. He became a captain at the tender age of 20 and spent some years in the West Indies, where he enforced British law a little too vigorously for the Admiralty, who refused to give him another command until war broke out with France in 1792. During this frustrating time, Nelson lived in Burnham Thorpe with his wife Frances (Fanny). Once back in service he was sent to the Mediterranean, but was blinded in his right eye by splinters from a parapet struck by enemy fire. Undaunted, he returned to duty the next day.

When he left the Mediterranean in 1797, Nelson's small fleet encountered a much larger French one. Due largely to his unusual tactics, the British were victorious, leading to a knighthood for Nelson. He lost his arm in the Canary Islands, trying to capture Spanish treasure, and was wounded again in the Battle of the Nile – from which he emerged victorious. He was then nursed by Emma, Lady Hamilton.

Nelson's brazen affair with Emma Hamilton (who became pregnant with their daughter Horatia) led to an estrangement from Fanny, and lack of money forced him to apply for active service again. His fleet engaged a hostile force near Copenhagen, where he refused to obey the order of a senior officer to disengage. The battle was won, along with further honours. Four years later, in 1805, he was fatally wounded at the Battle of Trafalgar.

There are many reminders of Nelson in the Burnhams. His bust stands above his father's tomb in All Saints' Church, along with flags from his battles, and flags and ensigns from the World War II battleship HMS *Nelson*.

Walk directions

❶ Find the Hero pub, then turn right, then immediately left down East Harbour Way until you reach

Walk information

Distance: 4 miles (6.4km) + extension 3½ miles (5.6km)
Map: OS Explorer 251 Norfolk Coast Central
Start/finish: on-street parking on main road in Burnham Overy Staithe; grid ref TF 844441
Ascent/gradient: 1
Paths: waymarked paths and some paved lanes; 1 stile
Landscape: wild salt marshes and mudflats, fields and meadows

Wooden rowing boats at low tide

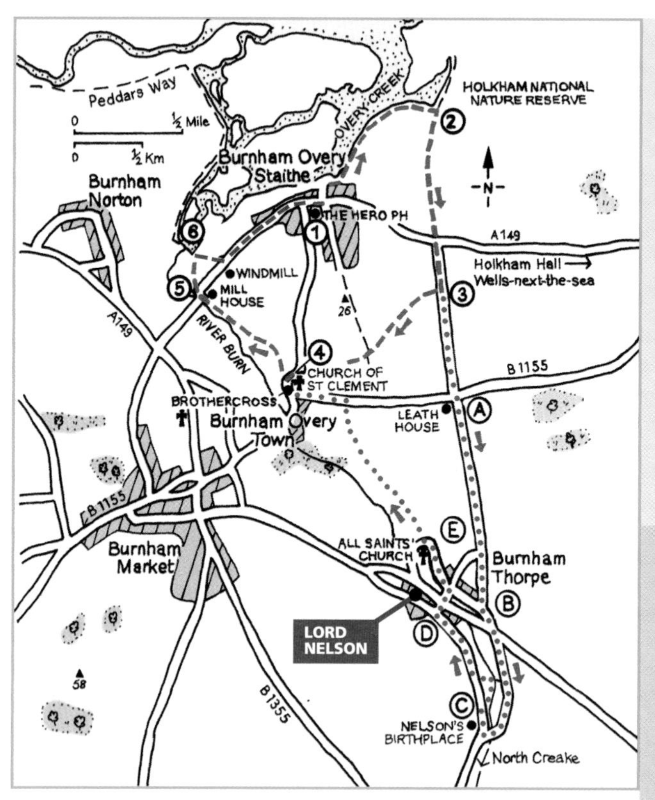

Overy Creek. Turn right next to the black-painted house, go through a gate and then bear left along the waterfront. The bank you are on was raised to protect the adjacent land from sudden incursions by the sea. Eventually, the path reaches a T-junction.

❷ At the junction, turn right, around the gate, into a marshy meadow of long grass. This area is part of Holkham National Nature Reserve and the sand dunes, salt marshes and mudflats are home to a wide variety of birds and plants, including plovers and sea aster. Cross a stile, then follow the grass track until you reach the A149. Cross to the track opposite, and follow this until you have passed two fields on your right.

❸ (The extension to Burnham Thorpe starts here.) Go through the gap at the entrance to the third field, which may or may not be marked as a footpath. Keep to the right until you reach a waymarker pointing left, across the middle of the field. Keep going in a straight line, through gaps in hedges, until you reach a dirt lane. Cross this and go down the track opposite, towards the Norman tower of Burnham Overy's Church of St Clement, which is topped by a 17th-century bell turret.

While there

You can explore the seven Burnhams – Market, Overy, Overy Staithe, Overy Town, Norton, Deepdale and Thorpe. Burnham Norton's church has a Saxon round tower, while Burnham Market has a handsome green, fringed by elegant 18th-century houses. Along the coast to the east is Holkham Hall with its Bygones Museum, while nearby Wells-next-the-Sea (which isn't really) is famous for its whelks and sprats.

Look for

In the marshes look for sea aster and samphire. In the summer months, you will also see the purple bloom of sea lavender. Besides wading birds that inhabit the salt marshes and mudflats all year, you will also see noisy Brent geese, with their characteristic black heads and white rumps, in the winter.

❹ Turn left at the end of the track onto Mill Road, then right up the track called Marsh Lane. Go through the gate and into a field, so that the River Burn is off to your left, with the round Saxon tower of Burnham Norton in the distance to your left and Burnham

Lord Nelson

Walsingham Rd, Burnham Thorpe PE31 8HN
Tel: 01328 738241
Directions: XX
Open: 11–3, 6–11 (Sun 12–3, 7–10.30; winter 11–2.30)
Bar meals: lunch and dinner served all week, 12–2, 7–9; average main course £9.95
Brewery/company: Greene King
Principal beers: Greene King Abbot Ale & IPA, Woodforde's Wherry Best
Children welcome. Dogs allowed
Parking: 30

***Step inside this** lovely, atmospheric 350-year-old cottage, which is known for its huge high-backed settles, old brick floors, open fires and traditional atmosphere. This unspoilt gem was named after England's most famous seafarer, who was born in the rectory of this sleepy village in 1758. Nelson memorabilia can also be seen in the pub. Greene King and Woodforde ales are tapped from the cask in the cellar room, or a dram of the popular rum concoction called 'Nelson's Blood', made to a secret recipe, can be sampled here.*

The food also makes a visit worthwhile, with its seafood, vegetarian choices, grills and baguettes: starters like chicken leg terrine with red onion marmalade, and star anise confit, might be followed by chicken and wild mushroom pasta bake, and braised lamb shank with tomato cassoulet.

Families are warmly welcomed here, and children can enjoy the garden with its climbing frame and wooden play area.

Overy windmill straight ahead. Go through the gate by Mill House, which dates from 1820.

5 Cross the A149, with the pond on your left, then take the public footpath into the next field. If the stile is too choked by brambles, use the main gate, but keep the hedge not too far from your right. In the distance you will see the sails of Burnham Overy windmill. Note: there's no fully passable direct route to Burnham Overy from this point.

6 At the junction of paths, turn right and continue for ½ mile (0.4km) to reach the A149 main coast road. Turn left and follow this back into the centre of Burnham Overy Staithe.

Extension to Burnham Thorpe

The River Burn is a placid stream that meanders slowly through its pretty little valley of meadows, dotted with sheep in the summer. Monks and friars obviously thought this was a good place to live, because two religious orders founded priories here.

The tranquillity of the valley was rudely shattered in 1953 and again in 1978, when north winds and high spring tides caused the sea defences to fail and water came rushing in. The result was devastating, with the river bursting its banks and flooding homes and farms.

Begin the extension at Point **3** and, instead of going across the field, continue down the lane towards Burnham Thorpe. Large fields stretch away on either side. When you reach the crossroads, with Leath House to your right, Point **A**, continue past the houses into a shady lane, with orchards to the left and right, shielded from the bitter sea winds by hedges.

Keep to the left at the first junction, and take the road towards North Creake at the second junction, Point **B**. Here are the best views of the valley of the River Burn. When you reach a tiny bridge, cross it and follow the sign to Nelson's birthplace, Point **C**, marked by a plaque on the wall. This was given to the village by one of his officers.

Take the footpath opposite the Parsonage to follow the river for a while, then rejoin the lane. On reaching Burnham Thorpe, go right on Gardeners Row, Point **D**, passing the **Lord Nelson** pub on the left. At the end of the street, cut across the green to the track that leads to All Saints' Church.

The rood in the chancel arch is made up of timbers from Nelson's flagship at Trafalgar, HMS *Victory*. Opposite the church, a footpath, Point **E**, leads through a kissing gate and across a meadow, with the river to your left. Eventually, the path reaches a lane. Turn left and walk into Burnham Overy Staithe, past the broken Brothercross, where villagers once traded their wares. Turn right at the junction, and rejoin the main route at Point **4**.

Walk information

Distance: 6 miles (9.7km)
Map: OS Explorer 227 Peterborough
Start/finish: Falcon Inn, Fotheringhay; grid ref TL 059932
Ascent/gradient: 2
Paths: field paths, tracks and bridleways, some road walking; 3 stiles
Landscape: low-lying water meadows, pasture and parkland

Water meadows at Fotheringhay

30: Through the water meadows of the Nene

Cross picturesque water meadows and pasture on this gentle walk by the River Nene.

Walk directions

❶ From the **Falcon Inn** turn right and take the turning opposite, signposted to Nassington. Cross the Willow Brook and take a waymarked footpath on the right to the far boundary, crossing into the next field by an oak tree. Follow the clear path diagonally right towards farm outbuildings.

❷ With the house facing you, veer right, then left alongside the buildings, keeping three trees over to the right in the field. Follow the clear path towards hedge and trees, making for the field's left-hand corner. Cross a wooden footbridge and aim diagonally across the field to a dismantled railway track. Cross over and follow a grassy track through the fields to a footbridge spanning the River Nene.

❸ Walk along to the next bridge and cross the river by Elton Lock. Make for the village green at Elton and turn right at the road. Turn right after a few paces into Chapel Lane and head out of the village, passing alongside Elton Park and some cottages and then continue on a bridleway. Cross a wooden footbridge and then ascend a slope towards trees. Make for a gate and join a track leading to a woodland path. Keep ahead.

❹ Emerge from the trees, follow the field edge to a mast in the corner, drop down the bank to a gate and turn right. Make for two kissing gates, cross the A605 to two more gates and then turn right in the field. Look for a stile in the boundary, with two gates just beyond it. Turn right and follow the road round to the left. Turn right at the Nene Way sign, pass under the A605 and keep right in front of Eaglethorpe Mill.

❺ Turn left immediately beyond it, cross a stile and veer away from the water to a stile and footbridge. Continue ahead to Warmington Lock. Veer slightly left towards Fotheringhay Church and join a track. When it bends right, go straight on along the field path to the next track. Turn left, pass sheep pens and head for the site of Fotheringhay Castle. Turn right here, follow the track and return to the **Falcon Inn.**

Falcon Inn

Fotheringhay PE8 5HZ
Tel: 01832 226254
Directions: *north of A605 between Peterborough and Oundle*
Open: *11.30–3, 6–11 (Sun 12–3, 7–10.30)*
Bar meals: *lunch and dinner served all week, 12–2.15, 7–9.30; average main course £9.50*
Restaurant: *lunch and dinner served all week, 12–2.15, 7–9.30; average 3 course à la carte £24*
Brewery/company: *free house*
Principal beers: *Adnams Bitter, Greene King IPA, Scottish Courage John Smith's, Nethergate*
Children welcome
Parking: *30*

An attractive 18th*-century stone-built inn set in a historic village close to the site of Fotheringhay Castle, where Mary, Queen of Scots, was beheaded in 1587. The garden was recently redesigned by landscape architect Bunny Guinness, with an extensive lawn overlooking Fotheringhay church.*

The Falcon and chef/patron Ray Smikle are members of the select Huntsbridge Inns group, each member producing innovative food in a relaxing pub environment. Eat what you like where you like, and accompany your meal with excellent wines or a pint of good ale. The choice is between the locals' tap bar, the smart rear dining room, or the conservatory extension, where you can then choose from the seasonal carte or blackboard snack selection. Crispy duck spring rolls with spiced Asian coleslaw, chorizo sausage salad, shank of lamb with colcannon, spinach and fried carrots, and couscous with roast Mediterranean vegetables and Feta cheese give some idea of the variety of dishes on offer.

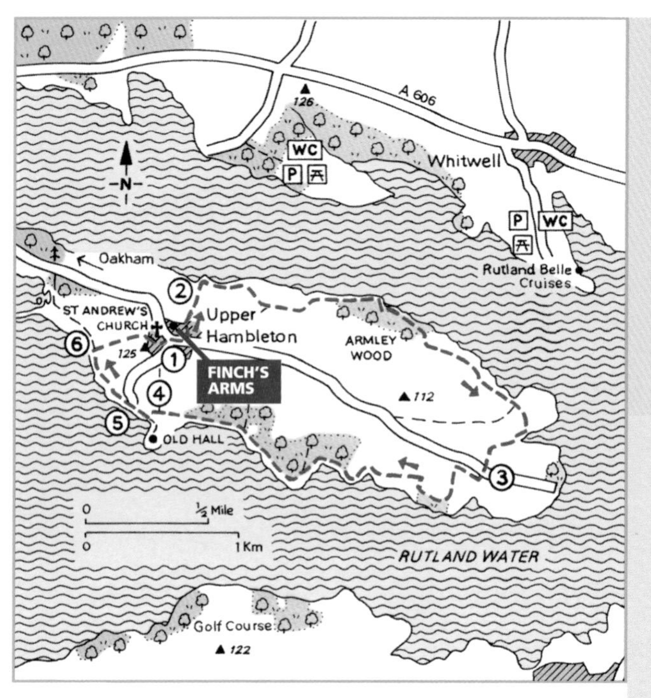

Walk information

Distance: 4½ miles (7.2km)
Map: OS Explorer 234 Rutland Water
Start/finish: roadside parking in Upper Hambleton; grid ref SK 900075
Ascent/gradient: 1
Paths: wide and firm the whole distance; several stiles
Landscape: low-lying peninsula of dipping fields and woodland

While there

Just to the south of Rutland Water is the picturesque village of Wing, where there is a most unusual historic maze. Cut into the roadside turf near the recreation ground, Wing Maze is based on an 11-ringed design often found on the floors of medieval French cathedrals. Wing itself once had a monastery, and it's possible that the monks may have followed the lines of the maze, stopping to pray at certain points.

31: A ramble by Rutland Water

Rutland Water's 3,100 acres (1,255ha) make it one of the largest artificial lakes in the whole of western Europe – and it's in England's smallest county.

Work began in 1973 with the flooding of the Gwash Valley, but Anglia Water's reservoir is about much more than simply the supply of drinking water. Sailing and windsurfing are very popular, while fishermen are to be found on the shores and out in boats in virtually all weathers. There are picnic sites along the northern edge, a museum at the preserved church at Normanton on the southern shore, and afternoon cruises on the *Rutland Belle* that plies the water daily between May and September. A 25-mile (40km) off-road cycling route encompasses the whole of Rutland Water.

Rutland Water is one of the most important centres for wildfowl in Britain – as many as 23,500 ducks have been recorded on a single winter's day, and a total of 250 different species of birds have been seen since 1975.

The nature reserve at the far western end of Rutland Water is managed by Leicestershire and Rutland Wildlife Trust, and at the Birdwatching Centre at Egleton you can obtain a permit to walk to the 15 hides that dot the secluded bays and lagoons.

Walk directions

❶ From the **Finch's Arms** pub in the centre of Upper Hambleton, walk eastwards on the long and level main street as far as the red pillar box. Turn left through the gate for the grassy lane, indicated 'public footpath', that leads straight through a gate and down the middle of a sloping field.

❷ Go through the gate at the bottom and turn right onto the wide track that runs just above the shore. This popular and peaceful route around the Hambleton peninsula is also shared by cyclists, so enjoy the walk but be alert. Follow it from field to field, and through Armley Wood, with ever-changing views across Rutland Water. As you gradually swing around the tip of the Hambleton peninsula with views towards the dam at the eastern end, you can begin to appreciate the sheer size of the reservoir, and how the birds, anglers, sailors and other users can all happily co-exist.

❸ When you arrive at a tarmac lane (gated to traffic at this point, since it simply disappears into the water a little further on!), go straight across to continue on the same unmade track. It turns right and runs parallel with the road a short distance, before heading left and back towards the water's edge and a lovely section of mixed woodland.

❹ Approaching Old Hall, a handsome building perched just above the shore, turn left to reach its surfaced drive, then go right and walk along it for 160 yards (146m) to reach a cattle grid.

❺ At this point you can return directly to Upper Hambleton by following the lane back uphill; otherwise veer left to continue along the open, waterside track, with views across to Egleton Bay and the corner of Rutland Water specially reserved for wildlife (out of bounds to sailing boats).

❻ After about 500 yards (457m) look for the easily missed stile in the hedge on your right, and the public footpath that heads straight up the field. (If you overshoot, or want to extend the walk by ½ mile (800m), simply carry on along the track to the very far end and return along the lane to the village.) Aim for the apex of the field, where successive stiles lead to a narrow passage between a hedge and a fence that eventually brings you out in the churchyard in the centre of the village, opposite the **Finch's Arms.**

Finch's Arms

Oakham Rd, Hambleton LE15 8TL
Tel: 01572 756675
Open: *10.30–3, 6–10.30*
Bar meals: *lunch and dinner served all week, 12–2.30, 7–9.30*
Restaurant: *lunch and dinner served all week, 12–2.30, 7–9.30; average 3 course £16*
Brewery/company: *free house*
Principal beers: *Greene King Abbot Ale, Scottish Courage Theakston, Theakston Best Bitter, Timothy Taylor Landlord*
Children welcome
Parking: *40*

Run by experienced *publicans Colin and Celia Crawford, this stone-built 17th-century inn, set in a sleepy village on a narrow strip of land jutting into Rutland Water, offers interesting Mediterranean-style food in a relaxed atmosphere. Once the pub would have looked out over a valley and the little village of Lower Hambleton, but these days it has stunning views over Rutland Water. Lower Hambleton has disappeared beneath its waters, but luckily for us Upper Hambleton and the Finch's Arms escaped this fate. During the time they have been here, the Crawfords have tastefully refurbished the pub, developing a stylish restaurant with cane furnishings and open fires, and the neat summer terrace.*

From inside and out diners can enjoy the views while tucking into bar snacks such as corned beef hash with fried eggs, smoked chicken with penne pasta, sun-dried tomato tart with basil pesto, and crisp Thai fishcakes on sesame noodles. There's often a set two-or three-course menu of the day, offering interesting dishes as well as good value. In the Garden Room, dishes are more ambitious: choose from starters such as duck liver, pancetta and truffle slice with cranberry chutney, or baked goats' cheese and figs wrapped in Parma ham with rosemary and tomato oil. Main selections might include roast breast of goose with sage and onion rösti, or perhaps medallions of pork on caramelised apple mash with parsnip crisps and honey and clove sauce.

32: The coast between Southwold and Walberswick

Southwold, situated on an island between the River Blyth and the sea, is one of those genteel, low key seaside resorts where everything is done in good taste.

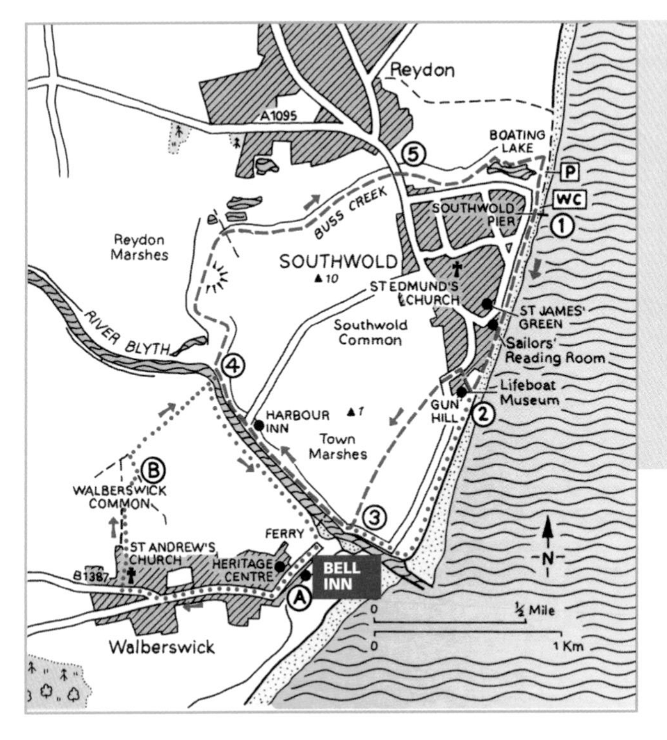

Make no mistake, this is a popular spot but it has none of the brashness of kiss-me-quick Felixstowe or Lowestoft. The character of Southwold seems to be summed up by the rows of brightly-coloured beach huts on the seafront promenade and the peaceful greens with their Georgian and Edwardian houses. The Adnams brewery dominates the town and it is no surprise to discover that the beer is still delivered to pubs on horse-drawn drays. Southwold is simply that sort of place.

The arrival of the first steamboats for more than 70 years marked a return to the glory days for Southwold Pier in the summer of 2002. The pier was originally built in 1899, when Southwold was a flourishing Victorian holiday resort. Mixed bathing had just been introduced on the beach, on condition that men and women were kept at least 20 yards (18m) apart and changed in separate 'bathing machines' into costumes which covered their bodies from neck to knees. The *Belle* steamer brought holidaymakers on its daily voyage from London and the pier was a hive of activity.

The T-end, where the boats docked, was swept away in a storm in 1934. During World War II, the pier was split in two as a precaution against a German invasion. By the time Chris and Helen Iredale bought the pier in 1987, storms and neglect had reduced it to a rotting hulk. Years later, the couple have realised their dream of rebuilding and

Walk information

Distance: 4 miles (6.4km) + extension ½ mile (0.8km), or 2 miles (3.2km) if no ferry
Map: OS Explorer 231 Southwold & Bungay
Start/finish: beach car park (pay-and-display), Southwold; grid ref TM 511766
Ascent/gradient: negligible
Paths: riverside paths, seaside promenade, town streets; 2 stiles
Landscape: Southwold and its surroundings – river, marshes, coast

reopening the pier, so that visitors can once again stroll along the boardwalk and watch the boats unloading their passengers at a new landing stage.

An exhibition on the pier tells the history of the seaside holiday, complete with saucy postcards, kitsch teapots, palm readers, end-of-the-pier shows, high-diving 'professors' and old-style arcade machines – such as the 'kiss-meter' where you can find out whether you are flirtatious, amorous, frigid or sexy. A separate pavilion contains modern machines by local inventor Tim Hunkin, who also designed the ingenious water clock, with chimes and special effects every half-hour.

Walk directions

❶ Leave the pier and turn left along the seafront, either following the promenade past the beach huts and climbing some steps or walking along the clifftop path with views over the beach. After passing St James' Green, where a pair of cannons stand either side of a mast, continue along the clifftop path to Gun Hill, where six more cannons, captured at the Battle of Culloden in 1746, can be seen facing out to sea.

❷ From Gun Hill, head inland alongside the large South Green, then turn left along Queen's Road to the junction with Gardner Road. Cross this road and look for the Ferry Path footpath, that follows a stream beside the marshes as it heads towards the river. Alternatively, stay on the clifftop path and walk across the dunes until you reach the mouth of the River Blyth.

❸ Turn right and walk beside the river, passing the Walberswick ferry (the extension starts here), a group of fishing huts where fresh fish is sold, and the Harbour Inn. After about ¾ mile (1.2km) you reach an iron bridge on the site of the old Southwold–Halesworth railway line (if no ferry, the extension starts here).

❹ Keep straight ahead at the bridge, crossing a stile and following the path round to the right alongside Buss Creek to make a complete circuit of the island. There are good views across the common to Southwold, dominated by the lighthouse and the tower of St Edmund's Church. Horses and cattle can often be seen grazing on the marshes. Keep straight ahead at a four-finger signpost and stay on the raised path to reach a white-painted bridge.

❺ Climb up to the road and cross the bridge, then continue on the path beside Buss Creek with views of beach huts in the distance. The path skirts a boating lake on its way down to the sea. Turn right and walk across the car park to return to the pier.

Extension to Walberswick

Turn right at Point ❸ and look for the landing stage, where a ferryboat shuttles back and forth across the river in summer. At various times this route has been served by a steamboat and a chain ferry, but these days you travel in an old-fashioned rowing boat for which you pay a modest charge. You may catch a glimpse of an old man and boy, waiting for the last ferry. The spectral couple are the ghosts of a pair who drowned whilst trying to cross the river. In winter, when the ferry does not operate, stay on the main route until you reach Point ❹, then cross the bridge and walk back along the path on the other side of the river.

While there

The Southwold Sailors' Reading Room on East Cliff was opened in 1864 in memory of Captain Rayley, a naval officer at the time of the Battle of Trafalgar. Although it retains its original purpose as a library and meeting place, it is now a small museum containing model boats, figureheads and portraits of local sailors and fishermen. Near by, on Gun Hill, a former coastguard look-out houses the tiny Lifeboat Museum, open on summer afternoons, with exhibits on the history of the Southwold lifeboats. Among the items to look for is a hand-operated foghorn, similar in appearance to a set of bellows.

Look for

It's worth a visit to the cathedral-like St Edmund's Church, whose 100-foot (30-m) flint tower stands guard over the town. The greatest treasure here is the 15th-century rood screen which spans the width of the church, a riot of colour as vivid as when it was first painted, with angels in glory and a set of panels depicting the twelve apostles.

On the opposite bank, keep straight ahead to walk along the Street through Walberswick. Pass the attractive **Bell Inn,** left, and come to the village green, Point Ⓐ, where a heritage centre, situated inside an old chapel, features displays on the history of the village. In the 15th century, this was a thriving port with a large fishing fleet. When the harbour silted up, Walberswick went into decline and it is only recently that it has discovered a new lease of life as an artists' colony. It's a popular trip for holidaymakers from Southwold who take the ferry and spend the afternoon browsing in its tea rooms, art galleries and antiques shops.

Stay on the Street as it bends right, and fork right at a junction to reach St Andrew's Church, built within the ruins of an earlier church which stands as a testament to Walberswick's changing history. Just beyond the church, turn right along Church Street and follow this lane to the end. Keep straight ahead on a path across Walberswick Common, an area of gorse and open heathland. When the path forks, keep right and follow this path to a concrete lane, Point Ⓑ.

Turn left and stay on this lane as it bends right on the old trackbed of the Southwold–Halesworth railway. Continue until you reach an iron footbridge, Point ❹ of the main walk. Cross this bridge and turn left to continue with the main route.

***Reputedly 600 years** old, the Bell is situated at the heart of Walberswick, close to the village green and a stone's throw from the beach and the ancient fishing harbour on the River Blyth. Its peace and tranquility have attracted many visitors over the years and its atmosphere on Suffolk's sweeping coast is timeless. The artists Charles Rennie Mackintosh and Philip Wilson Steer stayed at the Bell, the latter also lodging next door at Valley Farm. Montagu Rhodes James wrote one of the best-known ghost stories, 'Whistle and I'll come to you my lad', while staying here in 1929. To the north, across the River Blyth, is Southwold, a classic seaside town with a highly individual, old-fashioned air. Reach it either by foot or seasonal ferry. To the south lie the woodland heaths of Dunwich and the Minsmere Bird Sanctuary, while to the west is the famous 'Cathedral of the Marshes' at Blythburgh. Inside, the Bell's low beams, open fires, flagged floors and high wooden settles create a warm, homely welcome.*

Traditional English pub fare and a seasonal menu are the Bell's hallmarks. Among the perennial favourites are whole grilled plaice, beef stew and dumplings, mushroom Stroganoff, and chicken supreme. There is a good range of vegetarian dishes and sandwiches too, all to be washed down with well kept Adnams ales or a selection of wines.

Bell Inn

Ferry Rd, Walberswick IP18 6TN
Tel: 01502 723109
***Directions:** from the A12 take the B1387 to Walberswick*
***Open:** 11–3, 6–11 (Sat 11–11, Sun 12–10, and all day in summer)*
***Bar meals:** lunch and dinner served all week, 12–2, 6–9; average main course £7.25*
***Restaurant:** dinner served Fri–Sat, 6–9; average 3 course à la carte £16*
***Brewery/company:** Adnams*
***Principal beers:** Adnams Best, Broadside, Mayday Regatta*
***Parking:** 10*
Children welcome
Dogs allowed

Walk information

Distance: 5½ miles (8.8km) + extension 4½ miles (7.2km)
Map: OS Explorers 196 Sudbury, Hadleigh & Dedham Vale; 211 Bury St Edmonds & Stowmarket
Start/finish: Church Street car park, Lavenham; grid ref TL 914489 (on Explorer 196)
Ascent/gradient: 2
Paths: field-edge paths and tracks, some road walking
Landscape: rolling farmland and attractive town

The Guildhall, Lavenham

33: Lavenham, a magnificent medieval timbered town

Lavenham is the best-preserved medieval town in England.

During the 15th and 16th centuries Lavenham grew rich on the wool trade, exporting cloth to Europe, Africa and Asia. At one time its people paid more in taxes than those of Lincoln and York. Merchants and clothiers built the half-timbered houses that still attract visitors today.

The town is an open-air museum of medieval architecture. When the wool trade declined, nothing took its place, with the result that the town centre retains its medieval street plan: a network of lanes fanning out from the market square with its 16th-century cross. Entire streets, such as Water Street, are lined with crooked, half-timbered houses, delicately colour-washed in ochre, mustard and Suffolk pink. Look out for the pargeting, such as the Tudor rose and fleur-de-lis on the façade of the Swan Inn.

The artist John Constable went to school here, at the Old Grammar School in Barn Street. One of his friends was Jane Taylor, who wrote the nursery rhyme 'Twinkle, Twinkle Little Star' (1806) at nearby Shilling Grange.

But the biggest name in Lavenham's history has been that of the de Vere family. Aubrey de Vere was granted the manor by his brother-in-law, William the Conqueror. Four centuries later, John de Vere, 13th Earl of Oxford, led Henry VII's victorious army at the Battle of Bosworth in 1485. This was the final battle of the Wars of the Roses, and it was in thanks for his safe return that local merchants built the parish church of St Peter and St Paul. One of the largest parish churches in England, its 141-foot (43-m) flint tower dominates the skyline.

This walk combines a visit to Lavenham with a gentle country stroll. To give yourself time to explore the town, follow the main walk out into the fields on either side of a broad river valley before ending up at the market square where you can visit the Guildhall and the venerable **Angel Hotel.** For a longer walk, extend your stroll to reach two delightful villages to the north-east – and still be back at Lavenham in time for tea.

Walk directions

❶ Turn right out of the car park and walk down the hill into town. At the first junction, turn right

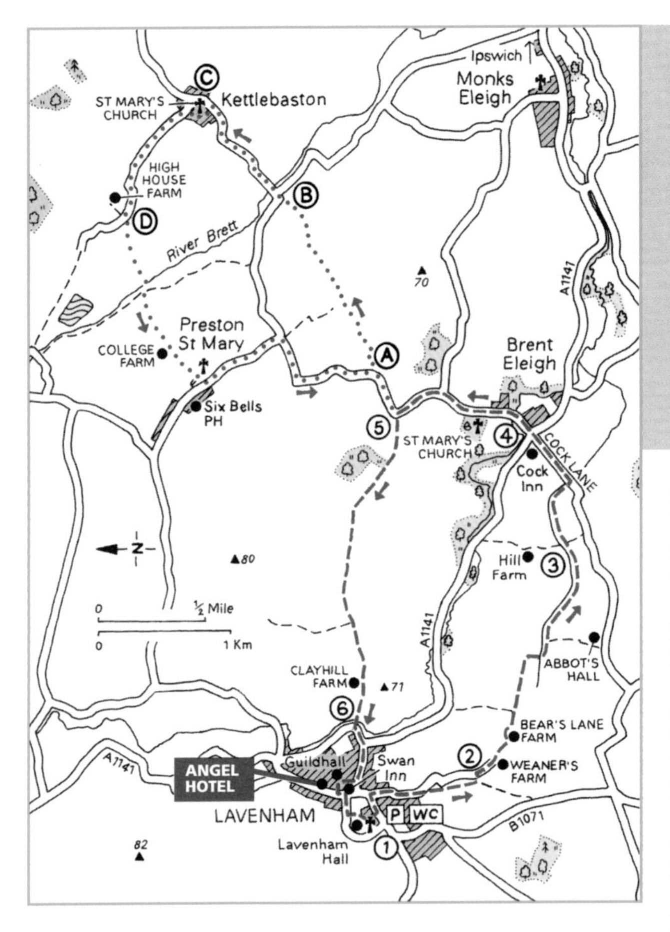

Look for

The village sign at Brent Eleigh, designed by a local artist in 2000, has aroused mixed feelings among villagers. It features a knight with helmet and shield, rising above some flames ('brent' means 'burnt', suggesting that a large fire took place here). Look for the tiny shamrock on the foot of the post – perhaps a sign that the artist was Irish

along Bear's Lane. Continue on this road for ¼ mile (400m) until the last house, then take the footpath to the right across the fields. After another ¼ mile (400m), reach a field boundary. Turn left across a small footbridge and follow a ditch to rejoin the road.

❷ Turn right and walk past Weaner's Farm, then turn left at a footpath sign just before a barn. Stay on this path as it swings around Bear's Lane Farm, then turn left onto a wide track beside a hedge. Follow this track as it drops down to the valley bottom. When the track bends right towards Abbot's Hall, keep straight ahead and fork to the right on a grassy path beside a stream.

❸ Emerging from a poplar grove, arrive at a concrete drive and turn right and immediately left. The path swings round to the right to reach a road, Cock Lane. Turn left and stay on this road as it climbs and then descends to a crossroads.

❹ Cross the A1141 into Brent Eleigh. Where the road bends, with the village hall and half-timbered Corner Farm to your right, keep straight ahead to climb to St Mary's Church. It's worth looking into the church to see the late 13th-century wall paintings and 17th-century box pews. Continue climbing up the same road. (The extension continues from here.)

❺ When the road swings sharply to the right, look for a path on the left. Stay on this path for 1¼ miles (2km) as it winds between tall hedges with occasional glimpses of open countryside. Emerging into the daylight, there is a wonderful view of the church tower at Lavenham. Walk past Clayhill Farm and descend into the valley, crossing a white bridge.

❻ Turn left at the junction and walk into Lavenham along Water Street, with its fine timber-framed houses. Just after De Vere House, turn right up Lady Street, passing the tourist office on the way to the market place (where you'll see the **Angel**, ahead). Turn left down narrow Market Lane to arrive at High Street opposite the picturesque Crooked House. Turn briefly left and then right along Hall Road. Before the road bends, look for a footpath on the left, then walk through a meadow to reach Lavenham church. The car park is across the road.

Extension to Kettlebaston

To extend the walk, keep to the road at Point ❺ as it swings round to the right. At the next bend, Point Ⓐ, turn right along a wide grassy track. There are fields on both sides at first, then a hedge, and eventually the track becomes a concrete lane. After 1 mile (1.6km) reach a road junction, Point Ⓑ. Keep straight ahead, cross a bridge and climb the hill into Kettlebaston.

St Mary's Church is Point Ⓒ. Opposite the church, the village sign features two crossed sceptres, one gold, the other ivory, topped by a pair of doves. This is a reference to William de la Pole, Marquis of Suffolk, who was granted the manor of Kettlebaston by Henry VI on condition that he bear a sceptre at all royal coronations. Turn left to enter the church through an arch of yews. At the back of the church are casts of the 14th-century Kettlebaston Alabasters, depicting the Coronation of Mary, the Annunciation, Ascension and Holy Trinity. The originals, discovered in the chancel wall in 1864, are now in the British Museum in London.

Walk through the churchyard and turn right behind the church, cross a meadow and climb over a stile to reach a lane. Turn left and walk along this lane for ½ mile (800m) between stud and cattle farms. Just before the entrance to High House Farm, Point Ⓓ, turn left on to a field-edge path running beside a ditch. At the foot of the field, cross two stiles and a wooden bridge to join a path on the other side of the stream. Follow this round to the right between paddocks, then cross a stile and walk uphill on a concrete lane to College Farm.

After passing the farm, the lane becomes a road leading into Preston St Mary. Look for a gap in the hedge on your left to enter St Mary's churchyard. Leave the churchyard at the far end and turn left onto the road.

Stay on this road, turning right along Whelp St to return to Point Ⓐ and rejoin the main walk at Point ❺.

Angel Hotel

Market Place, Lavenham
CO10 9QZ
Tel: 01787 247388
Directions: *from the A14 turn onto the A143 to take Bury East/Sudbury; after 4 miles (6.4km) take the A1141 to Lavenham*
Open: *11–11 (Sun 12–10.30)*
Bar meals: *lunch and dinner served all week, 12–2.15, 6.45–9.15; average main course £9*
Restaurant: *lunch and dinner served all week, 12–2.15, 6.45–9.15; average 3 course à la carte £17*
Brewery/company: *free house*
Principal beers: *Adnams Bitter, Nethergate, Greene King IPA & Abbott*
Children welcome
Parking: *105*
Rooms: *8 bedrooms en suite from s£50, d£75*

Originally licensed in *1420, this fine old inn stands amid some 300 listed buildings in the centre of England's best preserved medieval wool town. Despite its antiquity, the Angel assumes a thoroughly modern attitude to food in both the bar and dining room, and consistently attracts a loyal clientele. The food style is British with continental influences, using local suppliers for game, meat, vegetables and bread. Fresh fish is delivered daily. Lunchtime menus (except Sundays, when roasts are served) feature lighter meals such as home-made salmon fishcakes, and tomato, basil and Brie tart with salad. Home-made pickles and chutneys accompany home-made pork pies in summer, when lunch can also be taken in the garden. Main courses at other times might include pork and paprika casserole, and aubergine, black olive and spinach lasagne.*

Overnight accommodation is top-drawer for those who appreciate their creature comforts.

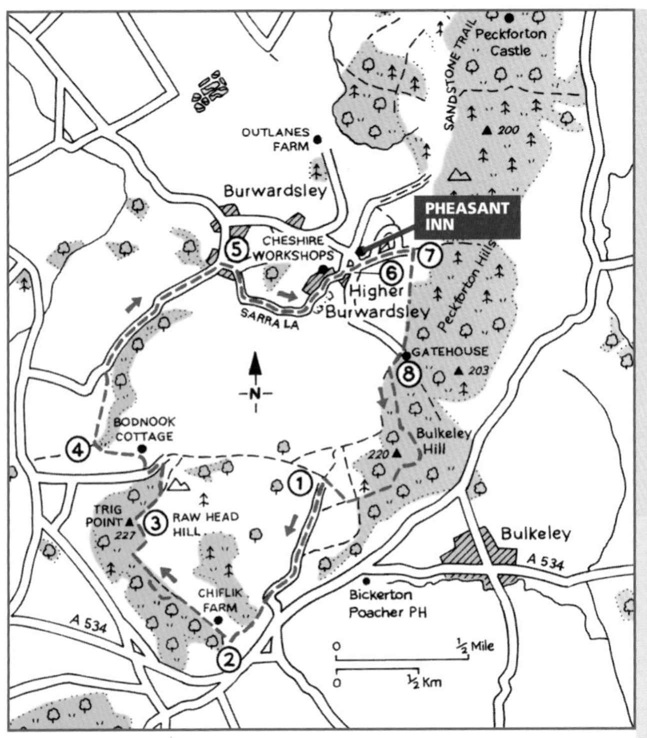

Walk information

Distance: 5½ miles (8.8km)
Map: OS Explorer 257 Crewe & Nantwich
Start/finish: Verges at end of tarmac on Coppermines Lane, Burwardsley, off A534; grid ref SJ 520550
Ascent/gradient: 2
Paths: field and woodland paths, some lane walking; 9 stiles (currently being replaced by gates)
Landscape: richly varied woodland and farmland, some rocky outcrops and views over lush plains

While there

Peckforton Castle isn't open to visitors, but Beeston Castle is – and to the elements too. Much of it is in ruins, apart from the gatehouse and some towers of the outer wall. Its condition seems perfectly fitting for the atmospheric site.

34: Castles in the air at Burwardsley

Enjoy a walk through wooded hills, with tantalising glimpses of two historic castles, and a pause for refreshment at a charming old country inn.

Beeston Castle, visible from afar, was built in the 13th century, but saw no real battles until the English Civil War around 400 years later. After changing hands several times, it was largely demolished in 1646 on Parliament's orders.

Nearby Peckforton Castle is a 19th-century imitation of a medieval fortress. Distant views of these castle-crowned ridges might lead you to anticipate airy ridge walking. In fact there's little of that to be found here – generally, this walk delivers something different and equally pleasurable.

From Coppermines Lane the way climbs to Raw Head Hill, along a steep slope which breaks into startling crags at Musket's Hole. The summit, at 746 feet (227m), is the highest point on the Sandstone Trail, a 34-mile (55km) route from Frodsham to Whitchurch. However, a screen of trees means it's far from the best viewpoint. The walk does serve up some great views, but never an all-round panorama: more a series of tasty morsels than a grand main course.

After Raw Head Hill the walk winds down through woods, fields and a quiet lane to Burwardsley village, then up to Higher Burwardsley. Then it climbs again to the National Trust-owned Bulkeley Hill Wood. The high point, literally and metaphorically, is a wonderful grove of sweet chestnut trees on a broad shelf rimmed by low sandstone crags. With virtually no undergrowth, you can fully appreciate the gnarled, multi-stemmed trees, which seem hunched with age. From here it's an easy stroll down through a plantation and then across a field back to Coppermines Lane.

Walk directions

❶ Walk down Coppermines Lane to a sharp left-hand bend, then cross a stile beside an arched sandstone overhang. Cross a field and ascend the edge of a wooded area. Cross fields to the edge of another wood. Go up right, joining a track towards Chiflik Farm.

❷ Go through a kissing gate by the farm and up a fenced path. The path generally runs just below the top of a steep slope, gradually climbing to the trig point on the top of Raw Head Hill.

❸ The path goes right and into a slight dip. Go left down steps then back right, slanting through a steep plantation. Go left down a narrow lane for 300 yards (274m). Opposite a track and footpath sign, descend right on clear ground under tall trees. At the bottom cross a stile and go up towards Bodnook Cottage. Just below this bear left and into a wood. Follow a much clearer path, roughly level, then slightly left and downhill among spindly beech trees.

❹ Cross a stile at the edge of the wood, then another immediately to its right. There's no path, so aim directly for a stile below a large tree, 50 yards (46m) left of a house. The path is clearer through the next field. At the end cross a stile and follow the road ahead.

❺ On the edge of Burwardsley village turn right up the first lane. Go right again up Sarra Lane, then fork left at an 'Unsuitable for Motor Vehicles' sign. Follow the lane through a narrow section then past Cheshire Workshops. Just beyond this the road forks.

❻ Go right (the **Pheasant Inn** is to your left), then straight on up the hill. Keep right at the next fork. The lane becomes unsurfaced at the Crewe and Nantwich boundary.

❼ Just before you get to the boundary sign go right over a stile and follow a clear path down the edge of a field. Keep straight on until you meet a narrow lane and go up left. On the crest, opposite a gatehouse, go right on a track.

❽ Go left up steps into the wood and continue less steeply. Where the path splits, the left branch follows the brink of a steep slope. Keep fairly close to this edge as the path levels. Go through a gap in a fence then descend straight ahead, through a plantation, to a kissing gate alongside a big iron gate. Go diagonally right on a clear track across a field back to Coppermines Lane.

Pheasant Inn

Burwardsley CH3 9PF
Tel: 01829 770434
Directions: *from Chester take the A41 to Whitchurch; after 4 miles (6.4km) turn left to Burwardsley; follow signs to 'Cheshire Workshops'*
Open: *11–11*
Bar meals: *lunch and dinner served all week, 12–2.30, 6.30–9.30; average main course £8*
Restaurant: *lunch and dinner served all week, 12–2.30, 6.30–9.30; average 3 course à la carte £18*
Brewery/company: *free house*
Principal beers: *Interbrew Bass, Weetwood Old Dog, Eastgate, Outhouse Best*
Children welcome
Parking: *40*
Rooms: *10 bedrooms en suite from s£55, d£70*

A traditional country *inn tucked away in a beautiful rural setting with lofty views of the Cheshire plain. Outside the delightful old sandstone building is a flower-filled courtyard ideal for summer evening drinks. The old outbuildings have been tastefully converted to provide a range of comfortable, modern bedrooms, each one individually decorated and furnished in contemporary styles. The half-timbered former farmhouse makes a great setting for a bar that boasts the largest log fire in the county.*

The proudest boast of all, however, is the food: home-cooked specialities might include starters of smoked haddock risotto or grilled black pudding, to be followed by twice-baked soufflé, poached halibut, or pork and apple sausage, with irresistable toffee and date pudding, or chocolate torte to finish.

35: A Lakeland walk for all seasons

Although it does include some steep sections this is not a particularly difficult walk, and there are outstanding views throughout its length.

The little lake of Elter Water and the petite Loughrigg Tarn are amongst the prettiest stretches of water in the region. The former, really three interconnected basins, was originally named Eltermere, which translates directly from the Old Norse into 'swan lake'. The swans are still here in abundance. The views over both lake and tarn, to the reclining lion profile of the Langdale Pikes are spectacular.

Each season paints a different picture. Golden daffodils by Langdale Beck in early spring, bluebells in Rob Rash woods in May, yellow maple in Elterwater village in October and a thousand shades of green, everywhere, all summer. The river is dominant throughout the lower stages of the walk. It starts as the Great Langdale Beck, before emerging from the confines of Elter Water as the sedate River Brathay. Ascent then leads to the suspended bowl of Loughrigg Tarn, followed by the open fell freedom of Little Loughrigg. This is very much a walk for all seasons, and should the section through the meadows by the Brathay be flooded, then a simple detour can easily be made onto the road to bypass the problem.

Walk directions

❶ From a start point close to the **Britannia Inn,** pass through a small gate to walk downstream above Great Langdale Beck. Continue to enter the mixed woods of Rob Rash. A little gate leads through the stone wall, the open foot of Elter Water lies to the right. Continue along the path through the meadows above the river. This section can be wet and is prone to flooding. Pass through the gate and enter mixed woods. Keep along the path to pass Skelwith Force waterfall down to the right. A little bridge leads across a channel to a viewing point above the falls. Keep along the path to pass through industrial buildings belonging to Kirkstone Quarry.

❷ Kirkstone Gallery is on the right, as the path becomes a small surfaced road. Continue to intercept the A593 by the bridge over the river where there are picnic benches. Turn left to pass the hotel. At the road junction, cross directly over the Great Langdale road to gain a lane which passes by the end of the cottages. Follow the lane, ascending to intercept another road. Turn right for a short distance and then left towards

Walk information

Distance: 4 miles (6.4km)
Map: OS Explorer OL 7 The English Lakes (SE)
Start/finish: National Trust car park (pay-and-display) at Elterwater; grid ref NY 328048
Ascent/gradient: 2
Paths: grassy and stony paths and tracks, surfaced lane; 4 stiles
Landscape: lake, tarn, fields, woods, open fellside, with views to the fells

Langdale Pikes and Elterwater

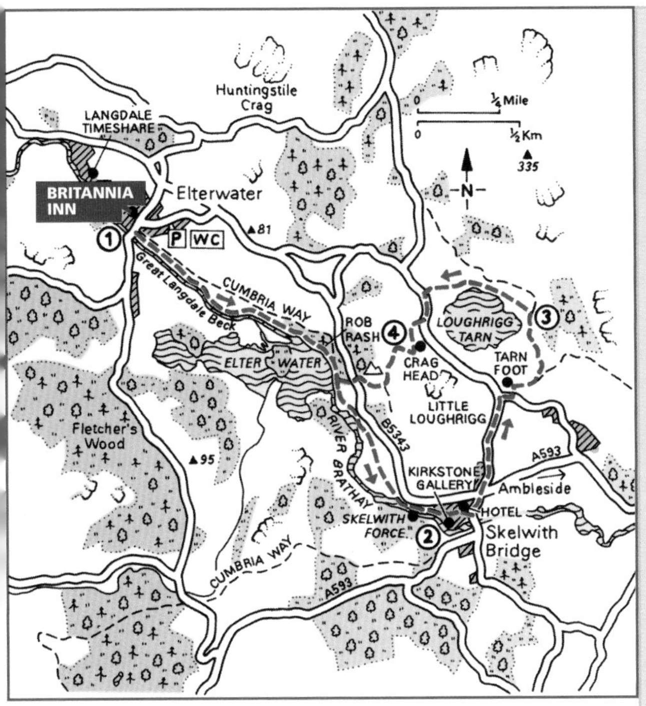

Tarn Foot farm. Bear right along the track, in front of the row of cottages. Where the track splits, bear left. Through the gate continue along the track to overlook Loughrigg Tarn. Halfway along the tarn cross the stile over the iron railings on the left.

3 Follow the footpath down the meadow to traverse right, just above the tarn. The footpath swings off right to climb a ladder stile over the stone wall. Follow the grassy track leading right, up the hill, to a gate and stile onto the road. Turn left along the road, until a surfaced drive leads up to the right, signed 'Public Footpath Skelwith Bridge'. Pass a small cottage and keep on the track to pass a higher cottage, Crag Head. A little way above this, a narrow grassy footpath leads off right, up the hillside, to gain a level shoulder between the craggy outcrops of Little Loughrigg.

4 Cross the shoulder and descend the path, passing a little tarn to the right, to intercept a stone wall. Keep left along the wall descending to find, in a few hundred paces, a ladder stile leading over the wall into the upper woods of Rob Rash. A steep descent leads down to the road. Cross this directly, and go over the little stone stile/broken wall next to the large double gates. Descend a track to meet up with the outward route. Bear right to return to Elterwater village and the **Britannia Inn.**

Britannia Inn

Elterwater LA22 9HP
Tel: 015394 37210
Directions: *take the A593 from Ambleside, then B5343 to Elterwater*
Open: *11–11 (Sun 12–10.30)*
Bar meals: *lunch and dinner served all week, 12–2, 6.30–9.30; average main course £8.95*
Restaurant: *lunch and dinner served all week, 12–2, 6.30–9.30*
Brewery/company: *free house*
Principal beers: *Jennings Bitter, Coniston Bluebird, Dent Aviator*
Children welcome
Dogs allowed
Parking: *10*
Rooms: *9 bedrooms, 8 en suite from s£60, d£76*

Overlooking the village *green in a famous scenic valley, the Britannia captures the essence of a traditional, family-run Lakeland inn. Originally a farmhouse and the premises of a local cobbler, the Britannia really comes to life in summer when colourful hanging baskets dazzle the eye and the garden fills up with customers and Morris dancers. Further away is the opportunity for energetic hikes and leisurely strolls amid Lakeland's glorious scenery.*

Lunches, afternoon snacks and dinner are served daily, with an extensive range of food and daily specials. Hearty home-made snacks include lamb rogan josh, Cumberland sausage and mash, quiche, and steak and kidney pie. The more ambitious evening menu might include steak Diane, and fresh bream with red and yellow pepper sauce.

Walk information

Distance: 8 miles (12.8km) + extension 7 miles (11.2km)
Map: OS Explorer OL 6 The English Lakes (SW)
Start/finish: car park at Ravenglass, close to station; grid ref SD 085964; Eskdale Green, grid ref SD 145998
Ascent/gradient: 3
Paths: clear tracks and paths (muddy after rain); 1 stile
Landscape: woodlands, moderately rugged fell, gentle valley

Sunset in Eskdale

36: Linking up with the Ravenglass & Eskdale Railway

This is a linear walk, but when the Ravenglass and Eskdale Railway is in full steam, a ride back on the train is simply a joy. It's also possible to return to Ravenglass using the extension walk.

Muncaster Fell is a long and knobbly fell of no great height. The summit rises to 758 feet (231m), but is a little off the route described. A winding path negotiates the fell from end to end and this can be linked with other paths and tracks to offer a fine walk from Ravenglass to Eskdale Green.

Affectionately known as La'al Ratty, the Ravenglass and Eskdale Railway has a history of fits and starts. It was originally opened as a standard gauge track in 1875 to serve a granite quarry, and was converted to narrow gauge between 1915 and 1917. After a period of closure it was bought by enthusiasts in 1960, overhauled and re-opened, and is now a firm favourite with visitors.

The line runs from Ravenglass to Dalegarth Station, near Boot at the head of Eskdale. The railway runs almost all year, but there are times in the winter when there are no services, so you should obtain a timetable and study it carefully in advance.

The Romans operated an important port facility at Ravenglass. Fortifications were built all the way around the Cumbrian coast to link with Hadrian's Wall and a Roman road cut through Eskdale, over the passes to Ambleside, then along the crest of High Street to link with the road network near Penrith. The mainline railway sliced through the old Roman fort in 1850, leaving only the bath-house intact, though even this ruin is among the tallest Roman remains in Britain. The Romans also operated a tileworks on the lower slopes of Muncaster Fell and the site is passed on the extension walk.

Surrounded by luxuriant rhododendrons, Muncaster Castle is almost completely hidden from view. It has been the home of the Pennington family since about 1240, though they occupied a nearby site even earlier than that. The estate around the castle includes a church that was founded in 1170, as well as a network of paths to explore. Owls are bred and reared at Muncaster, then released into the wild.

Walk directions

Leave Ravenglass by crossing ıe mainline and miniature ıilway line, using the footbridges rovided, then follow a narrow ath to a road junction. Turn right long a narrow road signposted Valls Castle'. The bathhouse is oon found on the left.

Continue along the access road nd turn left along a track ignposted 'Newtown Cottage'. urn left again before the cottage nd follow another track up a little vooded valley. Go through four ates, following the track from the vood, across fields and into nother wood. Turn left to reach lome Farm and a busy main road.

Cross the road and turn right, assing Muncaster Castle car park nd the Muncaster Guest House. he road leads up to a bend, vhere Fell Lane is signposted traight uphill. Follow the clear rack uphill, cross a little wooded ip, then fork right and left, oticing Muncaster Tarn on the ·ft. Go through a gate at the op of the lane to reach Muncaster Fell.

A path forges through boggy atches and bracken along the dge of a coniferous plantation, hen the path runs free across the ugged slopes of Muncaster Fell. A ath rising to the left leads to the ummit of the fell, otherwise keep ight to continue.

Views develop as the path vinds about on the slope verlooking Eskdale. A panorama f fells opens up as a curious tructure is reached at Ross's

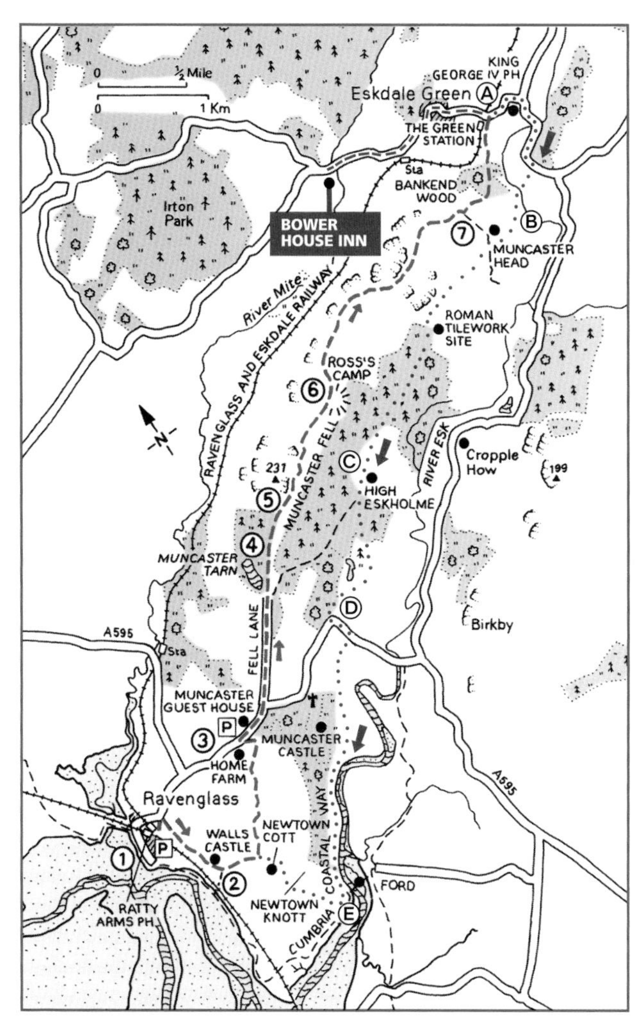

Camp. Here, a large stone slab was turned into a picnic table for a shooting party in 1883.

❻ Continue along the footpath, looping round a broad and boggy area to reach a corner of a dry stone wall. Go down through a gateway – take care, the path can be wet and muddy. There is a short ascent on a well-buttressed stretch, then the descent continues on a sparsely wooded slope, through a gate, ending on a track near another gate.

❼ Go through the gate and turn left, crossing a field to reach a stone wall seen at the edge of Bankend Wood. Keep to the right side of the wall to reach a stile and a stream. A narrow track

Look for

The Ravenglass estuary is a haunt of wildfowl and waders. Oystercatchers and curlews probe the mudflats and there are sometimes raucous flocks of gulls. On Muncaster Fell there may be grouse in the heather and it's usual to notice buzzards circling overhead.

While there

Don't forget to explore the little village of Ravenglass. It's essentially a fishing village at the confluence of the rivers Irt, Mite and Esk. Apart from being a Roman port, by 1280 it once had charters for a weekly market and annual fair. As trade diminished (eclipsed by the port of Whitehaven) it became a centre for rum smuggling.

continues, becoming better as it draws close to a road. Turn left at the end to reach the Green Station. Follow the road for 1 mile (1.6km) to the **Bower House Inn**.

Extension – walking back to Ravenglass

If there are no trains running back to Ravenglass, or for a longer walk, there is an easy route back to the sea. A good track leads along the lower slopes of Muncaster Fell, passing the site of an old Roman tileworks and a private golf course. The route links tracks and paths passing close to Muncaster Castle, weaving around the wooded estate and alongside the tidal reaches of the River Esk. The latter parts of the walk can be muddy in wet weather.

Walk from the Green Station, Point **A**, down the road to the King George IV pub. Turn right at a junction and follow the road over the River Esk. Turn right along an access road signposted 'Muncaster Head Farm'. The road crosses a stone bridge, dated 1889, which spans the River Esk, Point **B**.

After passing Muncaster Head Farm, you'll find there are two gates where the track forks. Keep to the right and follow the track into forest. Some parts have been felled and replanted. The Romans operated a tileworks to the left of the track, baking local mud. Reach an open area at High Eskholme, where there is a private golf course, Point **C**.

Shortly after passing High Eskholme, a sign points left through a gateway, indicating a public bridleway across the golf course. Walk alongside a strip of forest, through a gate, then along a clearer track. When a gate gives way to a broader track, turn right and follow it past a house and up to the busy main road, Point **D**.

Turn left down the main road, then right at a gatehouse to follow a clear track across fields. A Cumbria Coastal Way signpost points left along a woodland fence. (A diversion is signposted when herons are nesting.) Go through a gate and cross a footbridge, following a woodland path up to a track. Turn left down the track and walk beside the River Esk to reach a set of tide tables near a ford, Point **E**.

Just beyond this, turn right away from the river through a gate. Walk uphill through another gate in a wall, then follow a track to the left of Newtown Knott, to a gate at Newtown Cottage. Now retrace your earlier steps back to Walls Castle and Ravenglass.

Bower House Inn

Eskdale Green CA19 1TD
Tel: 019467 23244
Directions: *4 miles (6.4km) off the A595, ½ mile (0.8km) west of Eskdale Green*
Open: *11–11*
Bar meals: *lunch and dinner served all week, 12–2, 6.30–9.30; average main course £8.50*
Restaurant: *lunch and dinner served all week, 12–2, 7–8.30; average 3 course à la carte £22.50*
Brewery/company: *free house*
Principal beers: *Theakston Bitter, Jennings Bitter, Greene King Old Speckled Hen, Dent Ales*
Children welcome. Parking: *50*
Rooms: *25 bedrooms en suite from s£35, d£60*

This fine 17th*-century former farmhouse has a welcoming log fire and sheltered gardens overlooking Muncaster Fell. The oak-beamed bar and alcoves enhance the character of the place, and a charming candle-lit restaurant plays host to a varied selection of hearty, imaginative dishes.*

Cumberland wild duck, local pheasant in whisky, salmon with red pesto crust, and spinach and mushroom roulade may feature on the specials board, while the dinner menu may offer roast haunch of venison with red wine and juniper berry sauce, escalope of veal with ham and Gruyere, chicken breast with apple and tarragon sauce, or poached salmon in white wine and cucumber sauce.

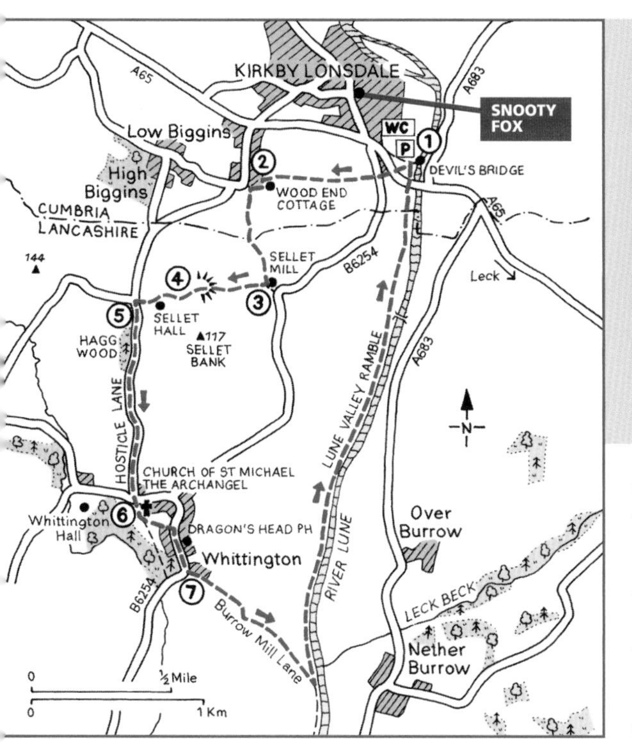

37: Through drumlin country from Kirkby Lonsdale

It's something of a revelation, to escape the weekend motorcycle congregation on Devil's Bridge and take this circular walk over rolling hills to Whittington.

You pass close to Sellet Mill; its huge waterwheel, incorporated within the building, was reputedly once the second largest in the whole country.

'Sellet' is an old local word for a drumlin, a small rounded hill formed by glacial deposits. The walk continues around the base of Sellet Bank (a large drumlin) and eventually to Sellet Hall. Built as a farm in 1570 by the Baines family, the hall may have been used at some time as a hospital, as it is situated at the end of Hosticle Lane – hosticle is an old dialect word for hospital. You return to Kirkby Lonsdale and the welcoming **Snooty Fox** pub along the banks of the River Lune. The river has inspired many artists, most famously J M W Turner, who visited Kirkby Lonsdale in 1818 and subsequently included the river in two of his paintings.

Walk information

Distance: 4¾ miles (7.7km)
Map: OS Explorer OL2 Yorkshire Dales – Southern & Western
Start/finish: Devil's Bridge car park, Kirkby Lonsdale; grid ref SD 615782
Ascent/gradient: 2
Paths: quiet lanes and tracks, overgrown and indistinct in patches; lots of stiles
Landscape: rolling hills, farmland, riverbank, good distance views

Walk directions

❶ From the west bank of the river, a few paces downstream from Devil's Bridge, take the path signposted 'Whittington' across a park with picnic tables to the A65. Cross over, go through a narrow meadow and between houses and almost immediately cross the B6254. As you enter another meadow, go uphill, keeping the walled wooded area on your left. Yellow markers and a sign to Wood End help locate the route. Keep on over the brow of the hill and straight ahead through two stiles. Turn left at another gap stile into the farmyard at Wood End Farm.

❷ Turn right on the farm track towards white-painted Wood End Cottage. Go left in front of the cottage along an overgrown,

Snooty Fox

One of a *trio of privately owned, well run country inns (along with the Mortal Man at Troutbeck and the Royal Oak in Appleby), the Snooty Fox is a listed Jacobean coaching inn at the centre of the town, the 'capital' of the scenic Lune Valley. Inside are roaring fires in rambling bars full of eye-catching artefacts. Beside a quaint cobbled courtyard is the pub's own herb garden, which signals its commitment to good food.*

A typical meal might start with duck liver and pistachio parfait, followed by roasted rack of lamb with spring onion mash and redcurrant jus. There are some inspiring fish dishes (steamed cod with sautéed potatoes, olives, crème fraîche and lumpfish caviar, or steamed huss wrapped in a banana leaf and served with a creamy saffron sauce) and plenty of prime condition ales to wash it all down. Well-appointed rooms promise a good night's sleep.

Main St, Kirkby Lonsdale LA6 2AH
Tel: 015242 71308
Directions: *from M6, junction 36, take the A65; the inn is 6 miles (9.6km) further on*
Open: *11–11 (Sun 12–10.30)*
Bar meals: *lunch and dinner served all week, 12–2.30, 6.30–9.30; average main course £7.50*
Restaurant: *lunch and dinner served all week, 12–2.30, 6–9.30; average 3 course à la carte £25*
Brewery/company: *free house*
Principal beers: *Theakston Best, Black Sheep, Timothy Taylor Landlord*
Children welcome
Dogs allowed
Parking: *12*
Rooms: *9 bedrooms en suite from s£36, d£56*

walled path down to Sellet Mill. A stream comes in from the left and tries to take over the path, but drier ground is just around the corner. The path opens out by the mill race with good views of Ingleborough over the water.

❸ Turn right by the cluster of homesteads and walk up the field, keeping the fence to your left, until level with the end of a garden. Go left through a yellow marked gate and walk straight across a small field to another marked gate, followed immediately by a shallow stream. Bear right to go round Sellet Bank, aiming initially for the corner of a hedge under a row of pylons. Continue with the hedge to your right, taking time to look back to Leck Fell and Barbon Fell.

❹ Go through a yellow marked stile on your right, then bear left round a wooded area. Facing Sellet Hall, turn right adjacent to the fenced driveway following the marker arrows, then keep on over the corner of the field to cross a stile and drop down a couple of steps to the road at a T-junction. Turn left along Hosticle Lane towards Whittington village.

❺ The tall trees of Hagg Wood are away on your right and hedges are beside you as you follow the lane down to Whittington.

❻ Go left at the T-junction for a few paces, then cross the road and turn right over a pebbled mosaic at the entrance to the Church of St Michael the Archangel. Keep the square bell tower on your left before descending stone steps to go through a narrow stile and the modern graveyard. Proceed through a gate in the left corner and cross straight over two small fields to a stone stile leading to a narrow, walled lane that leads on to Main Street. Turn right, in front of a lovely building dated 1875, and on through the village past the village hall and the Dragon's Head pub.

❼ At a sharp right bend on the edge of the village turn left along a sandy track, passing a farm and tennis courts. Follow the lane as it bends its way between fields to reach a pair of gates. Go through the gates on the left. Bear left to pick up the riverside walk – the Lune Valley Ramble – back to the A65 bridge at Kirkby Lonsdale. Go through a gate and up steps to the left of the parapet. Cross the road, drop down the other side to cross the park at the start of the walk.

38: A pastoral ramble and nature reserve

njoy this pastoral walk to the south-west of Kirkby Stephen, hrough Cumbria's wild Pennine country.

he route runs close to the River den and the scenic Settle–arlisle railway. The nature reserve n the walk – where more than o different species of bird have een identified – is owned by the **at Lamb** pub and managed nder a Countryside Stewardship greement.

Walk directions

❶ From the car park of the **Fat amb Country Inn,** walk towards Kirkby Stephen, crossing over both the cattle grid and Scandal Beck at the foot of the hill. Take the tarmac road to the right immediately beyond the bridge and follow it up over the fell to the farmhouse.

❷ Keeping the fields on your right, bear left, follow the path behind the house and continue across the fell, parallel with a wall. Look for a copse and head to the right of the trees. This is Jubilee Wood, planted to mark Queen Victoria's jubilee.

❸ Cross the old packhorse bridge on the far side of the wood to reach a road. This was once the

Walk information

Distance: 3½ miles (5.7 km)
Map: OS Outdoor Leisure 19 Howgill Fells
Start/finish: Fat Lamb, Cross Bank; grid ref NY 739023
Ascent/gradient: 2
Paths: roads, tracks and paths
Landscape: fields, fell and wood

The church at nearby Kirkby Stephen

Fat Lamb Country Inn

Crossbank, Ravenstonedale
CA17 4LL
Tel: 015396 23242
Directions: *on the A683 between Sedburgh and Kirkby Stephen*
Open: *11–2, 6–11*
Bar meals: *lunch and dinner served all week, 12–2, 6–10; average main course £7.50*
Restaurant: *lunch and dinner served all week, 12–2, 6–9; average 3 course à la carte £16*
Brewery/company: *free house*
Principal beers: *Cask Condition Tetley's Bitter*
Parking: *60*
Children welcome
Dogs allowed
Rooms: *12 bedrooms en suite from s£48, d£76*

The Fat Lamb *occupies a 17th-century farmhouse in magnificent countryside above the old market town of Kirkby Stephen. Located on high ground, the pub has been cut off by snow and once, when the inn was hosting a wedding reception, the bride-to-be sat alone, waiting patiently while her future husband battled in vain to get through the elements. The wedding was rescheduled and the bride travelled to church aboard a tractor, complete with white ribbons, before a second wedding breakfast at the Fat Lamb. Adjoining the pub is an 11-acre (4.45ha) nature reserve, home to interesting species of wildfowl.*

Chefs here use local produce whenever possible, and the varied bar-snack menu may offer home-made lasagne, best Whitby scampi, mixed sausage platter and a selection of cold platters. Bessy Beck trout with fennel and ginger butter sauce, and roast local leg of lamb with redcurrant jelly and mint gravy feature among the restaurant main courses.

main route between Sedburgh and Kirkby Stephen. Follow the tarmac road and bear right at a junction by some gates. Leave the road when it bears left and continue ahead down a track, to reach the main road at the bottom.

❹ Cross it and turn right for about 200 yards (183m) to a stile in the wall. Cross over and cut straight across the field, veering slightly to the right. Keep to the left of a small fenced enclosure and head diagonally across the far slope, bearing to the right, to the stile in the wall at the top. Walk straight ahead across the next field, crossing the stream by the bridge, and then veer towards the right side of the farmhouse ahead.

❺ Pass through the stile in the fa corner and turn right, keeping by the wall until you reach a gate leading over the bridge. Cross it and bear right by the side of the nature reserve to follow the waymarked route back to the **Fat Lamb** inn.

Walk information

Distance: 5 miles (8km) + extension 3 miles (4.8km)
Map: OS Outdoor Leisure 24 White Peak
Start/finish: Over Haddon car park (pay); grid ref SK 203657
Ascent/gradient: 984ft (300m)
Paths: generally well-defined paths; lots of stiles
Landscape: partially wooded limestone dales
Note: limestone dale sides can be slippery after rain

Tranquil Lathkill Dale

39: Meandering through the Derbyshire dales

'Lathkin is, by many degrees, the purest, the most transparent stream that I ever yet saw either at home or abroad...'

Charles Cotton, 1676

Today, when you descend the winding lane into this beautiful limestone dale, you're confronted by ash trees growing beneath tiered limestone crags, tumbling screes, multi pastel-coloured grasslands swaying in the breeze and that same crystal stream that Charles Cotton admired, still full of darting trout.

Yet it was not always so. In the 18th- and 19th-century lead miners came here and stripped the valley of its trees. They drilled shafts and adits into the white rock, built pump houses, elaborate aqueducts, water wheels and tramways; and when the old schemes failed to realise the intended profits they came up with new, even bigger ones. Inevitably nobody made any real money, and by 1870 the price of lead had slumped from overseas competition and the pistons finally stopped.

On this walk you will see the fading but still fascinating remnants of this past, juxtaposed with a seemingly natural world that is gradually reclaiming the land. In reality it's English Nature, who are managing these grasslands and woods as part of the Derbyshire Dales National Nature Reserve.

The walk starts with a narrow winding lane from Over Haddon to a clapper bridge by Lathkill Lodge. A lush tangle of semi-aquatic plants surround the river, and the valley sides are thick with ash and sycamore. In springtime you're likely to see nesting moorhens and mallard ducks. In the midst of the trees are some mossy pillars, all that remains of an aqueduct built to supply a head of water for the nearby Mandale Mine.

The path leaves the woods and the character of the dale changes markedly once again. Here sparse ash trees grow out of the limestone screes, where herb Robert adds splashes of pink. In the dry periods of summer the river may have disappeared completely beneath its permeable bed of limestone. The sun-dried soils on the southern slopes are too thin to support the humus-loving plants of the valley bottom. Instead, here you'll see the pretty early purple orchid, cowslips with their yellowy primrose-like flowers

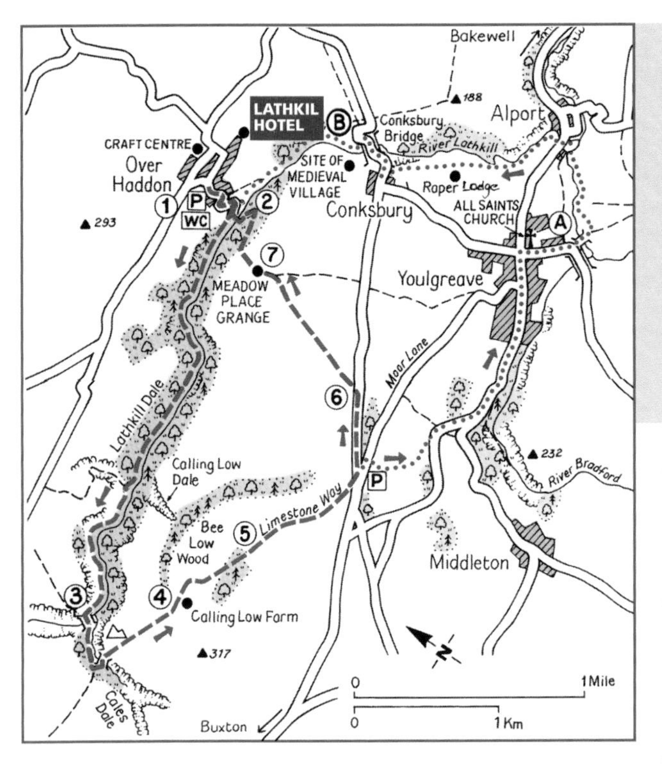

While there

Nearby Haddon Hall, home of the Dukes of Rutland, is well worth a visit. This 14th-century country house is as impressive as Chatsworth in its own way, with beautifully laid out gardens surrounding a Gothic-style main building. See the magnificent medieval Banqueting Hall, and the Long Gallery, with its Renaissance panelling.

and clumps of the yellow-flowered rock rose.

After climbing out of Cales Dale the walk traverses the high fields of the White Peak plateau. If you haven't already seen them, look out for Jacob's ladder, a 3-foot (1-m) tall, increasingly rare plant with clusters of bell-like purple-blue flowers. By the time you have crossed the little clapper bridge by Lathkill Lodge and climbed back up that winding lane to the car park, you will have experienced one of Derbyshire's finest dales.

Walk directions

❶ Turn right out of the car park, and descend the narrow tarmac lane, which winds down into Lathkill Dale.

❷ Just before reaching Lathkill Lodge and the river, turn right along a concessionary track that runs parallel to the north bank. The path passes several caves and a mineshaft as it weaves its way through woodland and thick vegetation. South of Haddon Grove the trees thin out to reveal the fine limestone crags and screes of the upper dale. The path now is rougher as it traverses an area of screes.

❸ Go over the footbridge and follow a little path sneaking into Cales Dale. Take the left fork down to a footbridge across the stream, which could well be dry outside the winter months. You now join the Limestone Way long distance route on a stepped path climbing eastwards out of the dale and onto the high pastures of Calling Low.

❹ The path heads east of south-east across the fields then, just before Calling Low Farm, diverts left (waymarked) through several small wooded enclosures. The path swings right beyond the farm, then half left across a cow-pocked field to its top left-hand corner and some woods.

❺ Over steps in the wall the path cuts a corner through the woods before continuing through more fields to reach a tarmac lane, where you turn left (the extension starts here).

❻ After about 500 yards (457m), follow a signposted footpath that begins at a stile in a dry-stone wall on the left. This heads north-east across fields to the huge farming complex of Meadow Place Grange. Waymarks show you the way across the cobbled courtyard, where the path continues between two stable blocks into another field.

.ook for

:alling Low Grange and
Aeadow Place Grange were
›nce farmed by monks – the
ormer by the Cistercian order of
:oche Abbey in Yorkshire, and
he latter by the Augustinian
›rder of Our Lady of Meadows
Leicester). The monks would
ıave tended sheep for the wool
rade. Today, both farms
oncentrate on dairy produce.

Lathkil Hotel

Over Haddon, Bakewell DE45 1JE
Tel: 01629 812501
Directions: *2 miles (3.2km) south-west of Bakewell*
Open: *11.30–3, 7–11 (11–11 Sat–Sun in summer)*
Bar meals: *lunch served all week, 12–2; average main course £6.50*
Restaurant: *dinner served all week, 7–9; average 3 course à la carte £20*
Brewery/company: *free house*
Principal beers: *Whim Hartington, Timothy Taylor Landlord, Wells Bombardier, Marston's Pedigree*
Children welcome
Dogs allowed
Parking: *28*

The Lathkill Hotel *was formerly the 'Miners Arms', named from the old lead mines in the area that date back to Roman times. An overnight stay here remains in the memory for the splendid panoramic views of the hills and dales of the Peak District from its Victorian-style bar.*

Home-cooked food has an enviable reputation locally, with a lunchtime hot-and-cold buffet in summer, and more extensive evening choices supplemented by cooked-to-order pizzas. Following onion bhajis with cucumber raita or tiger prawns in filo, indulge perhaps in a fruit sorbet before tackling sea bass with garlic and rosemary, Wootton Farm venison steak with Stilton sauce, or Barbary duck breast with blackcurrant coulis. More conventional steaks with optional sauces, and steak, kidney and oyster pie, along with a daily vegetarian dish, are regular alternatives. To follow, try the treacle tart, or toffee and apple crumble from the home-made puddings list, or perhaps cheese with biscuits.

❼ After heading north across the
ïeld to the brow of Lathkill Dale,
urn right through a gate onto a
ig-zag track descending to the
iver. Cross the old clapper bridge
o Lathkill Lodge and follow the
›utward route, a tarmac lane,
›ack to the car park and
efreshment at the well-placed
athkill Hotel.

:xtension to /oulgreave

ake a little more time in this area
ınd you'll find another beautiful
ıale and the village of
'oulegreave.

Follow the main route to the
oad beyond Point ❺. Instead of
urning left follow the right fork,
Aoor Lane, to the car park. From
ıere a track leads the route south
›efore swinging left down to
ınother road overlooking the
›leasantly wooded Bradford Dale.
ollow the road left into
'oulgreave, passing the youth
ostel, which is an old converted
:o-op building, and the George
Iotel to reach All Saints Church,
'oint Ⓐ. The church has a
ıagnificent Perpendicular tower
ınd a largely Norman nave. Inside is the alabaster tomb of Thomas Cokayne of Harthill Hall, who was killed in a brawl in 1488.

Turn right by the church and follow the road down towards the River Bradford. Where the road bends right, turn left on a track descending behind a house to a footbridge across the river. After crossing the footbridge turn left and trace the south bank beneath the woods and limestone cliffs of Rheinstor. The route crosses the river by a footbridge and continues to the road just west of Alport. The village, sited by the confluence of the Bradford and Lathkill rivers, has some lovely 17th- and 18th-century cottages.

Staggered right across the road, the next footpath begins at a stile, the first of many, and continues over fields and parallel to the River Lathkill. After passing beneath the gaunt mansion of Raper Hall the path meets Conksbury Lane, just west of Conksbury Bridge (Point Ⓑ), a packhorse bridge with medieval origins. The site of a medieval village lies on the hillside near Conksbury Farm.

Go over the bridge, then turn left on the path running alongside the Lathkill's east bank. After passing Lathkill Lodge, turn right to climb back up the tarmac lane to the car park at Over Haddon.

40: A riverside walk to the 'Meeting of the Waters'

Enjoy an attractive walk beside the sparkling River Greta, through a landscape that inspired the great writers Charles Dickens and Walter Scott.

Walk information

Distance: 5 miles (8 km)
Map: OS Outdoor Leisure 31 North Pennines
Start/finish: Morritt Arms, Greta Bridge; grid ref NT 084132
Ascent/gradient: 1
Paths: roads, lanes, field paths and riverside trails; several stiles
Landscape: banks of the River Greta, fields and woodland

Barnard Castle in County Durham.

Walk directions

❶ Turn right out of the venerable **Morrity Arms** hotel. Just before the bridge, cross the stile to go along the banks of the River Greta, then by a field side, and descend back to the river. Just over a mile (1.6km) along, through a wall opening, your path is to the right, signposted to Brignall village. (The ruins of St Mary's Church are a short detour straight ahead.)

The path ascends from the river to join a grassy path which leads past the vicarage and on to Brignall Church.

Morritt Arms

Greta Bridge, Barnard Castle
DL12 9SE
Tel: 01833 627232
Directions: *at Scotch Corner take the A66 towards Penrith; after 9 miles (14.4km) turn at Greta Bridge; the hotel is over the bridge*
Open: *7–11*
Bar meals: *lunch and dinner served all week, 12–3, 6–9.30; average main course £6*
Restaurant: *lunch and dinner served all week, 12–3, 7–9; average 3 course à la carte £25*
Brewery/company: *free house*
Principal beers: *Scottish Courage John Smith's, Theakston Best Bitter, Timothy Taylor Landlord, Black Sheep Best*
Children welcome
Dogs allowed
Parking: *100*

The present building *dates back to the 17th century when there was a farm on the site. Through the 19th century Greta Bridge became the second overnight stop of the London–Carlisle coaches. Over the years the outbuildings were incorporated into the hotel to create the stylish inn you will find today. Log fires warm the building in winter, and on balmy summer days you can eat out in the handsomely landscaped gardens.*

Food is served in the commemorative Dickens Bar (the author stayed here in 1839 while researching for Nicholas Nickleby*) as well as an informal bistro, Pallatt's, and the more formal Copperfield restaurant. Choose from bar snacks (from sandwiches to more hearty main courses such as sausages and mash, or steak and chips) through to restaurant specials such as pork fillet provençale with a rice timbale, or stir-fried duck in hoi sin sauce.*

❷ For a shorter walk, you can turn right here to go back down the road to the hotel. Otherwise, turn left and then right along the drive of 'Brookside'. The path goes through a gate and left of a farm building. Follow the yellow markers along the edge of two fields and then left to cross two steams running through a wooded dell. Go straight across the next field into woodland, then through another field to reach the A66.

❸ Cross the road with care to reach another church. Go through the churchyard and cross a stile, keeping the fence to your left. The path meets the main road by a stream. Cross the road and follow the stream, turning right to join the Teesdale Way.

❹ After emerging onto a private road, turn left. Follow the River Tees to the 'Meeting of the Waters', where it is joined by the River Greta. Cross the Dairy Bridge, follow the drive up to Mortham Tower and then follow the wall round to the left.

❺ After two stiles, head for a barn in the middle of the field. Turn right at the barn to rejoin the park wall and descend to an underpass by the river. Cross the field and then turn right to cross the arched bridge and return to the **Morritt Arms.**

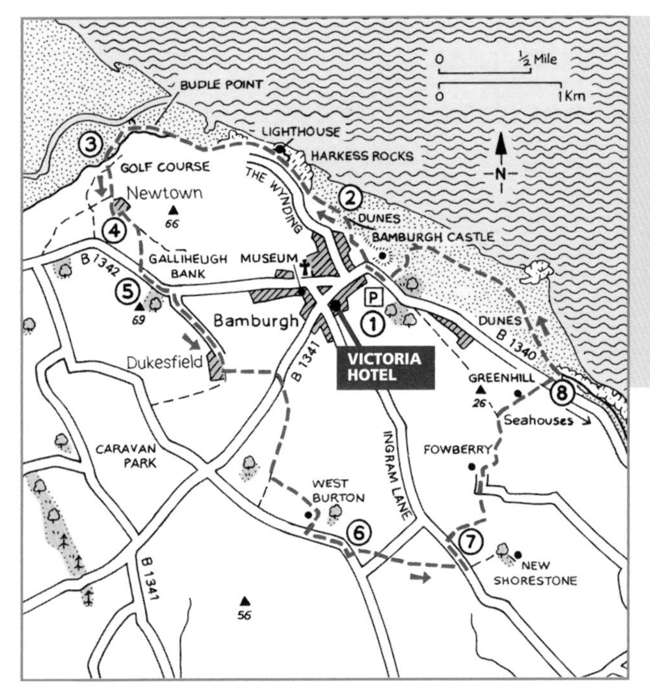

Walk information

Distance: 8½ miles (13.7km)
Map: OS Explorer 340 Holy Island & Bamburgh
Start/finish: by Bamburgh Castle (pay-and-display); grid ref NU 183348
Ascent/gradient: 2
Paths: field paths, dunes and beach; 10 stiles
Landscape: coastal pasture and dunes

41: A stirring tale of heroism on the Northumbrian shore

For as long as people have sailed this coast, the Farne Islands have been a hazard, claiming countless lives on their treacherous rocks.

The most easterly outcrop of Northumberland's whinstone intrusion, they form two main groups and comprise around 30 tilted, low-lying islands, some barely breaking the waves. In 1838 the wreck of the SS *Forfarshire* caught the imagination of the country because of the unstilted heroism of the Longstone lighthouse keeper, William Darling, and his daughter, Grace, in rescuing the survivors.

A storm was raging before dawn on 7 September when the *Forfarshire* struck Big Harcar, just south-west of Longstone. Grace was keeping watch with her father and spotted the wreck. At first light, they sighted men clinging to the wave-washed rock and launched their tiny coble to attempt a rescue. They found nine survivors, including a woman, but were only able to bring five back on the first trip. William returned with two of them for those remaining, whilst his daughter helped the others.

Grace became a national heroine, but remained unaffected by the publicity and stayed with her parents at Bamburgh. She died of tuberculosis just four years later at the age of 26. A museum on the green near the **Victoria Hotel** tells her story.

Walk directions

❶ Walk towards Bamburgh village, where you'll find the museum, the **hotel** and the church where Grace Darling is buried. Our route, however, continues along the beach, reached either across the green below the castle or by following the Wynding, just beyond, and then crossing the dunes behind.

❷ To the left, the sand soon gives way to Harkess Rocks. Pick your way round to the lighthouse at Blackrocks Point, which is more

Victoria Hotel

Front St, Bamburgh NE69 7BP
Tel: 01668 214431
Directions: *in the centre of Bamburgh, on the green*
Open: *11–11 (11–2 Fri & Sat)*
Bar meals: *lunch and dinner served all week, 12–3, 6–9; average main course £5.50*
Restaurant: *lunch served Sun, 12–3; dinner served all week, 7–9; average 3 course à la carte £20*
Brewery/company: *free house*
Principal beers: *John Smith's, Theakston's Cool Keg*
Children welcome
Dogs allowed.
Parking: *6*
Rooms: *29 bedrooms en suite from s£52.50, d£94*

Friendly, attentive service *is just one feature of this stylishly refurbished hotel, which overlooks Bamburgh's historic village green. The stone building is late Victorian, but the welcome is uncompromisingly modern. There's an airy candle-lit brasserie, a children's play den, and well equipped accommodation. The brasserie has a domed glass ceiling, a tiled floor and well spaced tables. Two real ales are always available in the popular bar.*

Both traditional and adventurous appetites are catered for: starters could include oak-smoked local salmon with a parsley and walnut pesto, or black pudding and toasted muffin stack served on a grain mustard honey dressing. For main courses expect the likes of pan-fried

Bamburgh sausages with aïoli mash and a carbonnade of onions, or fillet of beef with wild mushrooms and malt whisky jus, followed by appetising sweets or Northumbrian cheeses. Morning coffee and afternoon tea are also available.

easily negotiated to the landward side. Continue below the dunes, soon regaining a sandy beach to pass around Budle Point.

3 Shortly before a derelict pier, climb onto the dunes towards a World War II gun emplacement, behind which a waymarked path rises onto a golf course. Continue past markers to a gate, leaving along a track above a caravan park. At a bend, go through a gate on the left (marked 'Private') and carry on at the edge of the field to reach the cottages at Newtown.

4 Beyond, follow a wall on the left to regain the golf course over a stile at the top field-corner. Bear right to pass left of a look-out, and continue on a grass track to the main road.

5 Walk down Galliheugh Bank to a bend and turn off to Dukesfield. Approaching the lane's end, go left over a stile, walk past a house to the field's far corner and continue by a hedge to a road. Cross to follow a green lane opposite and eventually, just after a cottage, reach a stile on the left. Make for West Burton farm, turn right through the farmyard to a lane and then go left.

6 Beyond a bend and over a stile on the left, signed 'New Shorestone', bear half-right across a field. Emerging on to a quiet lane, go over another stile opposite and continue in the same direction to Ingram Lane.

7 Some 300 yards (274m) to the left, a gated track on the right leads away and then around to the left towards Fowberry. Meeting a narrow lane, go left to the farm, then turn right immediately before the entrance onto a green track. In the next field, follow the left perimeter around the corner to reach a metal gate. Go through that, and remain beside the right-hand wall to reach a double gate, there turning right across a final field to Greenhill. Keep ahead to the main road.

8 Continue across to the beach and head north to Bamburgh. Approaching the castle, turn inland, over the dunes, where a cattle fence can be crossed by one of several gates or stiles. Work your way through to regain the road by the car park.

42: Hiking around historic Hexham

It was AD 674 and the Romans had been gone over 200 years. Their mighty Hadrian's Wall lay crumbling on the green hills to the north, high above the valley of the Tyne.

These were the early days of Christianity, and the first monasteries and abbeys were being established. Queen Etheldra of Northumbria had given Bishop Wilfred the land by the river and here, at Hexham, he would build his priory.

Wilfred had travelled far and wide, including to Rome, and had been impressed by the splendour and majesty of many European churches. His would be a magnificent one, with 'crypts of beautifully finished stone... walls of wonderful height and length'. Many of the stones in his great building were Roman, removed from the fort at Corbridge. The monastery became a cathedral and a renowned centre of learning.

However, these were dark days and places like Hexham were rich pickings for Viking raiders. The priory was to be attacked on many occasions, and in AD 875 Halfdene the Dane, who had ransacked much of the county, finally burned it down. Although attempts were made, it wasn't until 1113, when the Augustinians were awarded the land and started the present abbey, that it was restored to its former majesty.

The abbey buildings survived Henry VIII's dissolution of the monasteries of the 1530s because they were was also used as a parish church. Instead of being demolished, Hexham was embellished and extended. The original crypt was retained intact too, and is now one of the finest Saxon structures to be found in Britain. While the nave and transepts date back to the 12th and 13th centuries, the east end and nave were constructed between 1850 and 1910.

In the shadow of the abbey, and also constructed with the

Look for

St Wilfrid's Seat, a 1,300-year-old frith (sanctuary) stool from the original priory, was sculpted from a block of stone and survived the Danish attacks. Some believe it to have been the coronation throne of the early Northumbrian kings, though it may have been a bishops' throne. Find it in the middle of the choir in Hexham Abbey.

Walk information

Distance: 3¾ miles (6km) + extension 1¾ miles (2.8km)
Map: OS Explorer OL43 Hadrian's Wall
Start/finish: car park by supermarket (pay-and-display); grid ref NY 939641
Ascent/gradient: 2
Paths: town streets, lanes and woodland paths; 4 stiles
Landscape: market town and small wooded valleys

Hexham grew up around its fine abbey

While there

Great Chesters, known to the Romans as Cilurnum and set on the banks of the North Tyne near Chollerford, is a wonderfully preserved Roman cavalry fort with a fine museum founded by archaeologist John Clayton.

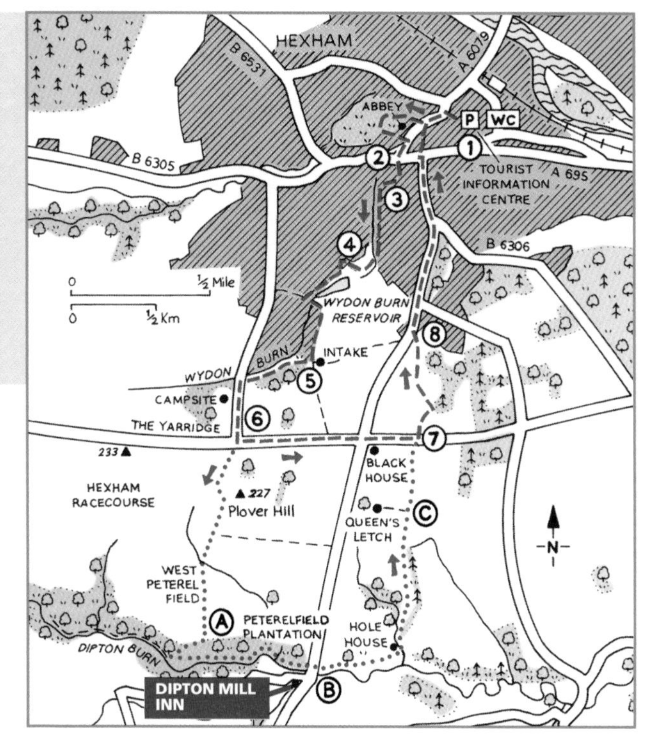

help of Roman masonry, are the 14th-century Moot Hall and the Manor Office, which was the first purpose-built gaol in Britain. The two buildings are the first points of interest you'll see on the walk.

Through the arch of the Moot Hall you come to the Market Square, which in 1761 became the scene of a major tragedy. Angry lead miners from Allendale, who were objecting to their conscription to the local militia, descended on Hexham in protest. On this spot they were read the Riot Act. Fighting broke out and, by the end of the day, over 300 miners were injured and 50 had been killed. The North Yorkshire Militia, who were responsible for the atrocity, were subsequently known as the Hexham Butchers.

Past Benson's Monument the walk comes to the edge of the old part of town and side-steps most of the new by climbing the southern hillsides along a wooded dell, known as Cowgarth Dene. The little stream here provided water for the monks of the priory. At the ominously named Black House you're at the top of the walk and can see Hexham and the valley that Wilfred inherited.

Walk directions

❶ From the car park (not the supermarket end) take the exit between the tourist information centre and the café to follow a narrow street past the Old Gaol. Go under the arches of the Moot Hall and enter the Market Place. Take a tour of the Sele, the park grounds surrounding Hexham Abbey, before aiming roughly south-west across them to the Queen Hall on Beaumont Street.

❷ Turn right along here to reach Benson's Monument, then continue straight ahead on an unnamed street. After taking the first turning on the right ignore Elvaston Road on the left, and instead go straight ahead on a tarred lane that leads to the foot of the wooded Cowgarth Dene.

❸ When you get to a bridge, turn off into the woodland where the now unsurfaced track crosses a footbridge and climbs out to a little park at the edge of a modern housing estate. Follow the woodland edge, then a track past a water treatment works.

❹ On nearing a housing estate, go through a gate on the left, then double back left on a path by some houses. Where the path turns right, climb some steps on to a track that runs along the north side of Wydon Burn Reservoir, now filled with reeds and tall grasses, not water.

❺ Turn left along the lane then, at Intake farm, turn right along a path that leads into the thick woods of Wydon Burn's upper reaches. A narrow path continues through the woods to reach the lane at Causey Hill. Turn left here past the campsite to reach a junction with a road known as the Yarridge. The modern building here is part of Hexham Racecourse. (The extension to the walk starts here.)

❻ Turn left along the road and go straight ahead at the crossroads.

❼ Beyond Black House a stile on the left marks the start of a downhill, cross-field path into Hexham. Beyond a step stile the path veers right to round some gorse bushes before resuming its course alongside the left field edge.

❽ Just before reaching a whitewashed cottage, go over the stile on the left and follow the road down into the town. Turn left along the shopping street at the bottom, then right along St Mary's Chare, back to the Market Place.

Dipton Mill Inn

Dipton Mill Rd, Hexham
NE46 1YA. Tel: 01434 606577
Directions: *2 miles (3.2km) south of Hexham on B6306 to Blanchland*
Open: *12–2.30, 6–11 (Sun 12–4, 7–10.30)*
Bar meals: *lunch and dinner served all week, 12–2.30, 6.30–8.30; average main course £5.45*
Brewery/company: *free house*
Principal beers: *Hexhamshire Shire Bitter, Devil's Water, Devil's Elbow, Whapweasel, Old Hembury*
Children welcome
Parking: *14*
Note: *no credit cards*

Originally part of *a farmhouse, the inn has been here since the 1800s. Enjoy a delightful walk through the woods to Hexham racecourse and back before relaxing with a pint of home-brewed Hexhamshire ale in the low-ceilinged bar.*

Freshly prepared food utilises ingredients from local suppliers; thus the bread rolls are made by a local baker, and the inn offers a good selection of local cheeses. Sample tomato and orange soup, followed perhaps by chicken breast in sherry sauce, or lamb steak in a wine and mushroom sauce, from the enterprising menu.

Extension to Hexham Common

This route goes a bit further, to the fringe of Hexhamshire Common, a low-lying area of heather moor that stretches out to the western edge of Northumberland and to the **Dipton Mill Inn.**
Leave the main walk at Point ❻. Across the road go over a ladder stile and follow a path across the first of many fields. The Hexham (National Hunt) Racecourse circuit and its buildings lie to the right. Through a gateway, cut diagonally left across the second field to a step stile in the boundary fence. The path heads south across two more fields, then follows an unsurfaced lane to the farm at West Peterel Field. Now you can see the Hexhamshire hills, which rise from the long, narrow wooded dene of Dipton Burn.

Beyond the farm the path follows a fence on the right as it descends towards the dene. After crossing a stile in the last field, the path changes to the other side of the fence, before raking down into the woods. At the far end of a clearing, double back along a clear track which soon re-enters the woodland of the Peterelfield Plantation, Point Ⓐ. There are many paths through the woods – stay with the main one that never strays too far from the burn. It emerges at the roadside close to ivy-clad Dipton Mill Inn (Point Ⓑ) – an ideal stop for lunch.

Across the road follow a track past an old mill building before continuing along a burnside path. At the paddocks, ignore the gate on the left but follow the perimeter path over the stile on the right – a recent diversion. Opposite Hole House turn left, following the path to the right of the cottage. Bear left over a footbridge, then climb through woodland.

At the top gate the route climbs across fields at the woodland edge then continues north past Queen's Letch (Point Ⓒ), a derelict farm. The Battle of Hexham Levels had ended in defeat for the Lancastrians. Queen Margaret of Anjou was fleeing with Edward, Prince of Wales, when her horse slipped on these slopes (a letch meant a slip in those times). They were befriended by a robber, who guided them to the Queen's Cave, 2 miles (3.2km) upstream.
Meet the road at Point ❼, east of Black House farm and follow the main route back to Hexham.

43: In Priestley's footsteps through Wharfedale

Literary pilgrims visit Hubberholme to see the George Inn, where novelist and critic J B Priestley (1894–1984) could often be found enjoying the local ale, and the churchyard, the last resting place for his ashes, as he requested.

He chose an idyllic spot. Set at the foot of Langstrothdale, Hubberholme is a cluster of old farmhouses and cottages surrounding the church. Norman in origin, St Michael's was once flooded so badly that fish were seen swimming in the nave. One vicar of Hubberholme is said to have carelessly baptised a child Amorous instead of Ambrose, a mistake that, once entered in the parish register, couldn't be altered. Amorous Stanley used his memorable name later in life as part of his stock-in-trade as a hawker.

Hubberholme church's best treasures are of wood. The rood loft above the screen is one of only two surviving in Yorkshire. Once holding figures of Christ on the Cross, St Mary and St John, it dates from 1558, when such examples of Popery were fast going out of fashion. It retains some of its once-garish colouring of red, gold and black. Master-carver Robert Thompson provided almost all the rest of the oak furniture in 1934 – look for his mouse trademark on each piece.

Yockenthwaite's name, said to have been derived from an ancient Irish name, Eogan, conjures up images of the past. Norse settlers were here more than 1,000 years ago – and even earlier settlers have left their mark, a Bronze Age stone circle a little further up the valley. The hamlet now consists of a few farm buildings beside the bridge over the Wharfe at the end of Langstrothdale Chase, a Norman hunting ground which used to have its own forest laws and punishments.

You walk along a typical Dales limestone terrace to reach Cray, on the road over from Bishopdale joining Wharfedale to Wensleydale. Here is another huddle of farmhouses, around the White Lion Inn. You then follow the Cray Gill downstream, past a series of small cascades. For a more spectacular waterfall, head up the road from the inn a little way to Cray High Bridge.

Walk information

Distance: 5 miles (8km) + extension 2¾ miles (4.4km)
Map: OS Outdoor Leisure 30 Yorkshire Dales – Northern & Central
Start/finish: by river in Hubberholme, opposite church (not church parking); grid ref SD 927782
Ascent/gradient: 2
Paths: field paths and tracks (steep after Yockenthwaite); 11 stiles
Landscape: streamside paths and limestone terrace

Dry stone walls, Wharfedale

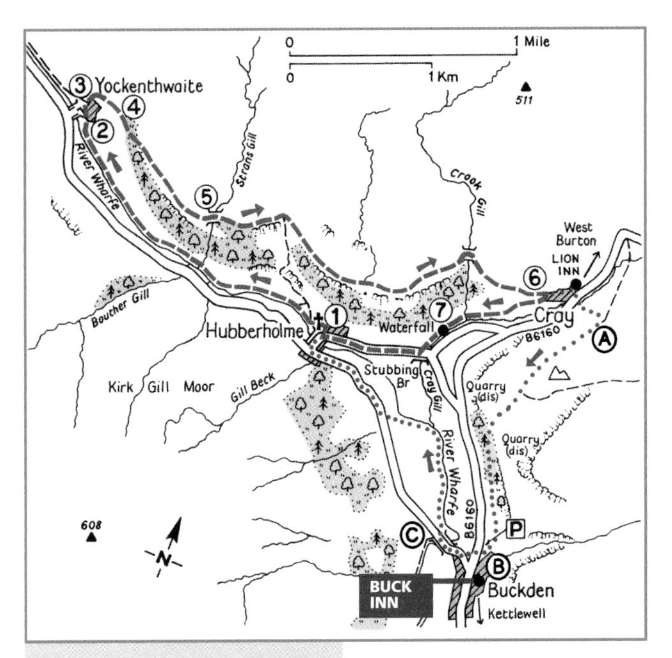

While there

If you've the energy, a walk to the summit of nearby Buckden Pike will reward you with fine views and a memorial to five Polish airmen whose plane crashed there in November 1942. One man survived the crash, following a fox's footprints through the snow down to safety at a farm. The cross he erected has a fox's head set in the base as thanksgiving. Buckden Pike is best climbed up the track called Walden Road from Starbotton.

Back in Hubberholme, the George Inn was once the vicarage. It is the scene each New Year's Day of an ancient auction. It begins with the lighting of a candle, after which the auctioneer asks for bids for the year's tenancy of the 'Poor Pasture', a 16-acre (7.2-ha) field behind the inn. All bids have to be completed before the candle burns out. In the days when the George housed the vicar, he ran the auction. Today a local auctioneer takes the role, and a merry time is had by all. The proceeds from the auction go to help the old people of the village.

Walk directions

❶ Go through a Dales Way signed gate near the east end of the churchyard, bend left and then take the lower path, signed 'Yockenthwaite'. Walk beside the river for 1¼ miles (2km) through three stiles, a gate and two more stiles. The path eventually rises to another stone stile into Yockenthwaite.

❷ Go through the stile and bend left to a wooden gate. Continue through a farm gate by a sign to Deepdale and Beckermonds. Before the track reaches a bridge go right and swing round to a sign to Cray and Hubberholme.

❸ Go up the hill and, as the track curves right, continue to follow the Cray and Hubberholme sign. Part-way up the hill go right at a footpath sign through a wooden gate in a fence.

❹ Go through a second gate to a footpath sign and ascend the hillside. Go through a gap in a wall by another signpost and follow the obvious path through several gaps in crossing walls. Go over two stone stiles and ascend again to a footbridge between two stiles.

❺ Cross the bridge and continue through woodland to another stile. Wind round the head of the valley and follow the signpost to Cray. Go over a footbridge. The footpath winds its way down the valley side. Go through a gate and straight ahead across meadowland to a gateway onto a track, and on to a stone barn.

❻ (The extension to the **Buck Inn** begins here.) Bend to the right beyond the barn, down to a public footpath sign to Stubbing Bridge. Go down the path between stone walls, through a wooden gate and onto the grassy hillside. Pass another footpath sign and continue downhill to meet the stream by a waterfall.

❼ Continue along the streamside path through woodland. Go over a wooden stile and on past a barn to a stone stile onto the road. Turn right along the road back to the parking place in Hubberholme.

Extension to Buckden

You can see more of the beautiful Upper Wharfedale scenery by extending the main walk to the peaceful village of Buckden, and the welcoming **Buck Inn.** At Point 6 on the main walk, continue straight ahead along the track and wind between the farm buildings to reach a metalled road by the White Lion Inn.

Cross the road and go over the stepping stones, then pass through a gate. Go straight ahead uphill to a signpost, and bend left, following a wall. At the top of the hill follow the wall as it diverts right to a gate, just beyond which is a signpost to Buckden, Point A.

Turn right along the path, which bends right; go over a stile and then through a gate by a large boulder. You are now on Buckden Rake, possibly the remains of a Roman road built by the army of Julius Agricola to link the fort at Ilkley in Wharfedale (possibly the Roman outpost of Olicana) to Virosidum (Bainbridge in Wensleydale). The grassy path becomes a stony track and goes downhill through a wooden gate and into woodland.

Descend into Buckden car park and go straight ahead by the 'No Exit' sign onto the main road by the Buckden Village Restaurant, Point B.

Buckden, always a strategically important point in the Dales, is an attractive estate village at the junction of several roads and tracks. It was a centre from which the Norman and medieval noblemen set out to hunt deer in the Langstrothdale Forest; the **Buck Inn** is a reminder of this ancient tradition.

The village is dominated by Buckden Pike, 2,304 feet (702m) high, to the north-east. Cross the road and follow the track beside the green. Turn right along the road and over the bridge. A few paces beyond, go over a gated stile on the right, signed 'Hubberholme', Point C.

Go over three wooden stiles, and eventually swing away from the riverside to reach a road. Turn right back to Hubberholme, turning right over the bridge back to the church and the parking place.

Buck Inn

Buckden BD23 5JA
Tel: 01756 760228
Directions: *from Skipton take the B6265, then B6160*
Open: *8–11*
Bar meals: *lunch and dinner served all week, 12–5, 6.30–9; average main course £8.50*
Restaurant: *dinner served all week, 6.30–9; average 4 course à la carte £23.95*
Brewery/company: *free house*
Principal beers: *Theakston Best, Black Bull & Old Peculiar, Scottish Courage John Smith's*
Children welcome
Dogs allowed
Parking: *40*
Rooms: *14 bedrooms en suite from s£36, d£72*

The Buck is *an inn for all seasons, facing south across the village green, in an unspoilt corner of the Yorkshire Dales. The old Georgian coaching inn is backed by the famous hill of Buckden Pike, and surrounded by picturesque stone cottages and panoramic views. Real ales are hand-pulled at the cosy bar.*

A wide choice of imaginative dishes is served in the pretty restaurant, where the daily changing choice is based on Dales meat, fresh fish and local vegetables. Start with the likes of breaded fishcake with deep-fried leeks, and move on to confit of roast lamb shank with olive mash, redcurrant and mint gravy. Save space for warm treacle tart with ginger ice cream.

44: Where the lead miners toiled

The quiet villages of Arkle Town and Langthwaite are grey clusters of houses in the austere splendour of Arkengarthdale.

One of the most northerly of the valleys in the Dales, it runs northwards from Swaledale into dark moorland, with the battle-scarred Stainmore beyond its head. This isolation and stillness is deceptive, however, for until the beginning of the 20th century the surrounding hills were mined for lead. The metal was first dug here in prehistoric times, but industrial mining of the great veins of lead really began in the 17th century. By 1628 there was a smelt mill beside the Slei Gill, which you will pass on the walk, and it is possible to pick out the evidence of some of the early miners' methods.

Booze (Norse for 'the house on the curved hillside') is now just a cluster of farm buildings, but was once a thriving mining community with more than 40 houses. You'll pass the spoil heaps of Windegg Mines, before returning to the valley near Scar House, now a shooting lodge but once belonging to the mine master. Near Eskeleth Bridge is the powder house, a small octagonal building, set safely by itself in a field. Built about 1804, it served the Octagon Smelt Mill, the remains of which can be traced near by. Just after you turn right along the road are the ruins of Langthwaite Smelt Mill. Lord of the Manor Charles Bathurst held the mining rights here for much of the 18th century.

Walk directions

❶ Leave the car park, turn right, then right again into Langthwaite village. Go over the bridge and continue ahead between cottages. Climb the hill and follow the lane to the hamlet of

Walk information

Distance: 8 miles (12.9km)
Map: OS Outdoor Leisure 30 Yorkshire Dales – Northern & Central
Start/finish: car park (pay-and-display) at south end of Langthwaite; grid ref NZ 005024
Ascent/gradient: 3
Paths: mostly clear tracks, some heather moor; 4 stiles
Landscape: mining-scarred moorland, with evocative remains of industry

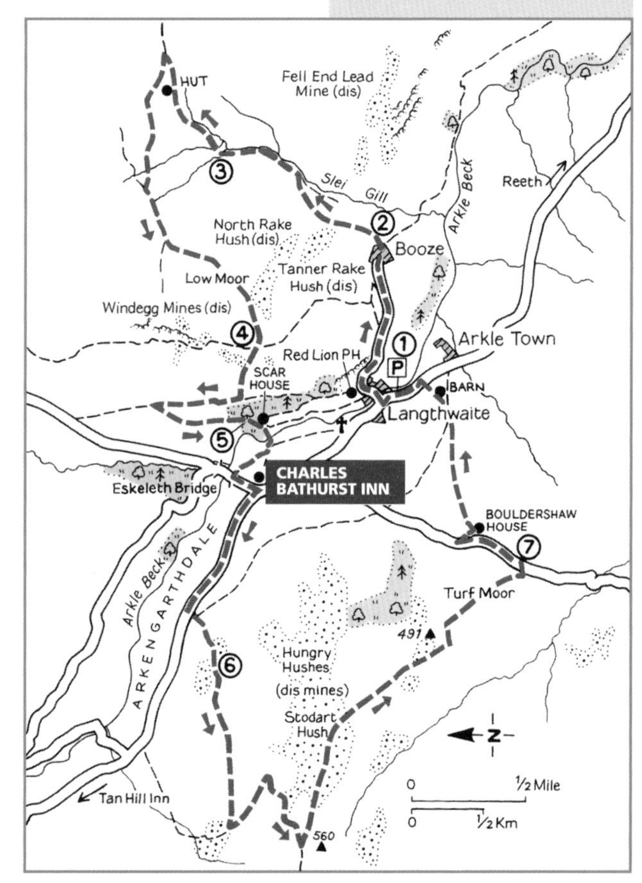

Booze. Pass the farmhouse and a stone barn and follow the track to a gate.

❷ After the gate, where the track bends left, go straight on next to a broken wall. Bear right to go past a ruined cottage, then follow the path to the stream. Walk upstream, go through a gate and then cross the stream on the stepping stones.

❸ Walk slightly left, through the moorland, to reach a wooden hut near a crossing track. Turn left along the track. At a crossing of tracks go straight on, then at a T-junction turn left. Where the wall on your right ends, leave the track, bending right along a path and down to a gate in the corner of two walls.

❹ Follow the small gully downhill and go through a gate onto a track. Turn right along the track and continue through a gateway and onto another track by a barn. Follow this track as it bends left by a stone wall and then passes farm buildings. Go through two gates to reach a third, white gate.

❺ Go through the white gate to enter the grounds of Scar House. Follow the drive as it bears right, downhill, go over a bridge and cattle grid at the bottom, then turn right. Follow the track to a road. Turn left, uphill, to reach a T-junction, with the **Charles Bathurst Inn** on your left. Turn right and follow the road. After a cattle grid, turn left along a signed track.

❻ At a gravelled area bear right and continue uphill on the track. Where it divides, go left beside spoil heaps and pass the junction of two flues. The track winds uphill, right then left, to reach a T-junction of tracks. Turn left and follow the track downhill to reach a road.

❼ Turn left along the road. Just after a farmhouse turn right at a bridleway sign, which takes you towards the house; turn left before reaching it and follow the signed track. Go through a gate and continue downhill. Before a small barn, turn left. Go over four stiles to reach the road. Turn left back to the car park.

Look for

Dry-stone walls are a typical feature of Arkengarthdale, as in much of the Yorkshire Dales. There are around 4,680 miles (7,530km) of such walls in the National Park, many of them built during the enclosure of former common land in the 17th to 19th centuries. These are the ones that head straight as an arrow for the fell tops. Earlier walls tend to enclose smaller fields and were built from rocks gathered from the fields – some may date from earlier than 1000 BC. A lack of skilled wallers slows down the work of modern repair.

Charles Bathurst Inn

Arkengarthdale, Richmond
DL11 6EN
Tel: 01748 884567
Open: *11–11*
Bar meals: *lunch and dinner served all week, 12–2, 6.30–9*
Restaurant: *lunch and dinner served all week, 12–2, 6.30–9*
Brewery/company: *free house*
Principal beers: *Scottish Courage John Smith's Bitter & Smooth, Black Sheep Best, Riggwelter*
Parking: *50*
Rooms: *18 bedrooms en suite from s£45, d£65*

Located in glorious *Arkengarthdale, the most northerly of the Yorkshire Dales, this tastefully refurbished 18th-century hostelry is known throughout the area as the 'C B Inn'. The pub is named after the son of Oliver Cromwell's physician, who once owned lead mines in Arkengarthdale. The bar was once a hay barn and stable for the horses of guests. It looks very different today, and what strikes new visitors to this delightful inn is how busy it gets. The re-opening of the Charles Bathurst has transformed the local community, so much so that the pub now employs 30 people, all of whom are local.*

Enjoy excellent fresh fish, locally produced fruit, vegetables and meat – and the C B Inn specialises increasingly in local Swaledale lamb. Dishes on the ever-changing menu may feature five-fish fishcake, shank of lamb on lentil potato cake with juniper jus, and (in season) roast grouse with ham and horseradish sauce.

Accommodation is available in individually designed, en suite bedrooms with some dramatic views.

45: To the heart of the Kingdom of Dalriada

Follow the Crinan Canal along the southern fringe of Moine Mhor, the Great Moss, one of the last wild, raised bogs in Britain.

Moine Mhor is 13 feet (4m) in depth and is protected as part of a National Nature Reserve. It's a birdwatchers' paradise echoing with the distinctive cry of the curlew as it returns to breed each spring. Stonechats, resident year round, are joined by whinchats in summer and you may spot the odd osprey hunting fish in the River Add. Watch, too, for hen harriers quartering the moss in search of a meal. In different seasons the bog changes colour as heathers and grasses bloom then fade away. Cranberries bear purple flowers in the spring and deep red berries in autumn. Carnivorous plants like the bright green sundew plants lie in wait to catch unsuspecting insects in their sticky hairs.

In AD 500 the Scotti tribe from Antrim landed here and made the vast rock of Dunadd, in the middle of this great bog, the capital of the first Kingdom of Dalriada. Near the summit are rock carvings including the figure of a boar, which may have been the tribe's emblem, and some faint lines of ogam inscription. A basin and footprint carved into the rock were probably part of early coronation ceremonies.

Walk directions

❶ From the car park go down some steps, cross the road and turn left. Keep going until you reach a white cottage on your right. Turn right and onto a dirt

Walk information

Distance: 8¼ miles (13.3km)
Map: OS Explorer 358 Lochgilphead & Knapdale North
Start/finish: Dunardry Forest car park; grid ref NR 824908
Ascent/gradient: 176ft (55m)
Paths: canal towpath, country roads, farm tracks
Landscape: bog, hillside and pasture

Look for

Look for the remains of a boathouse beside locks 9 and 10. This is where the Linnet was kept during the winter months. She was a little steamer used to ferry holiday visitors along the canal. At Bellanoch look to see how the engineers cut the canal into the hillside when it proved impossible to lay a foundation on the Moine Mhor.

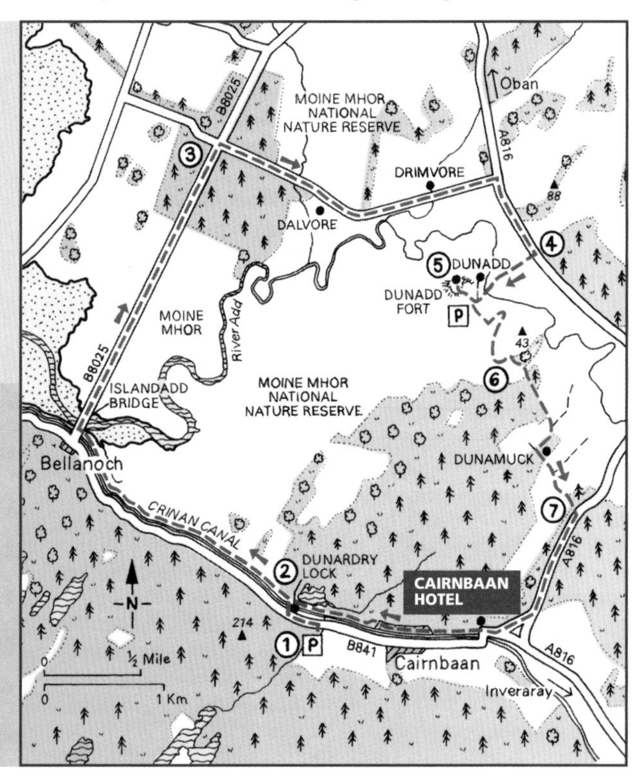

track that runs behind the cottage, then go through a gap between the fence and a wall. Cross the canal at Dunardry Lock and turn left onto the towpath.

❷ Head along the towpath as far as Bellanoch Bridge, then turn right onto the road, cross Islandadd Bridge and on to the B8025. This narrow, but not busy, road is long and straight and runs right through the Moine Mhor. Keep going for 2 miles (3.2km), then turn right onto a road signed to Drimvore.

❸ Follow this for about 1¾ miles (2.8km) as it runs through the National Nature Reserve and passes the farms of Dalvore and Drimvore. Finally reach a junction with the A816 and turn right. After ½ mile (800m) a Historic Scotland fingerpost will point you in the direction of Dunadd Fort.

❹ Turn right here onto a long, straight farm road and keep on it, passing the farm of Dunadd, to reach the car park. Make your way towards the hill on a well-trodden path, go past the house on the left and through a kissing gate. Continue on the path, following the directions arrows, to emerge through a gap in some rocks within the outer ramparts.

❺ Continue from here to the summit, then return by the same route to the car park. Leave it and turn right onto a farm track. Go through a gate then, almost immediately, go left through another gate and follow it as it curves left.

❻ Another gate is encountered just before the road turns right and heads uphill. Continue following the road going through another gate until you reach Dunamuck farm. Turn left through the steading, go through a gate and head downhill on a farm road, to meet the A816.

❼ Turn right onto the road and follow it for about ½ mile (800m), then turn right onto a road signposted to the **Cairnbaan Hotel.** After ¼ mile (400m) turn right onto the B841 and pass the hotel. As the road turns left across the swing bridge, keep straight ahead onto the canal towpath. Follow this to Dunardry Lock and retrace your steps to the car park.

Cairnbaan Hotel & Restaurant

Cairnbaan, Lochgilphead
PA31 8SJ
Tel: 01546 603668
Directions: *2 miles (3.2km) north of Lochgilphead on the A816, turn off onto B841*
Open: *11–11*
Bar meals: *lunch and dinner served all week, 12–2.30, 6–9.30; average main course £9*
Restaurant: *dinner served all week, 6–9.30; average 3 course £28*
Brewery/company: *free house*
Principal beers: *Bass*
Parking: *50*
Rooms: *12 bedrooms en suite from s£69.50, d£88*

Built in the *late 18th century as a coaching inn to serve fishermen and 'puffers' trading on the Crinan Canal, this hotel now offers smart accommodation and high standards of hospitality. The bedrooms are all furnished and decorated to individual designs, and provide the ideal opportunity to explore this lovely area. Visitors need not roam far from the hotel to seek their pleasure, however. You can watch the world go by on the canal, or enjoy a meal in the serene restaurant.*

The carte specialises in the use of fresh local produce, notably scallops, langoustines and game. Loch Etive mussels are likely to appear on the starter menu, along with smoked salmon and smoked trout pâté, while mains like breast of pheasant with haggis en croûte, lobster served thermidor or cold with mayonnaise, and fillet of halibut are guaranteed to revitalise any jaded palate. The choice of daily specials might include loin of tuna with pesto sauce, wild mushroom Stroganoff, or tenderloin of pork in sweet ginger. For a lighter meal from the bistro-style menu served in the lounge bar and conservatory, try fishcakes, or grilled goats' cheese to begin, then Cairnbaan fish pie, or perhaps chicken Madras, followed by profiteroles drizzled with warm chocolate sauce.

Walk information

Distance: 4½ miles (7.2km) + extension 3½ miles (5.7km)
Map: OS Explorer 351 Dunbar & North Berwick
Start/finish: main street, East Linton; grid ref NT 591772
Ascent/gradient: 2
Paths: field paths, river margins and woodland tracks, short section of busy road; 2 stiles
Landscape: cultivated fields, lively river and picturesque village

Right: ruined Hailes Castle

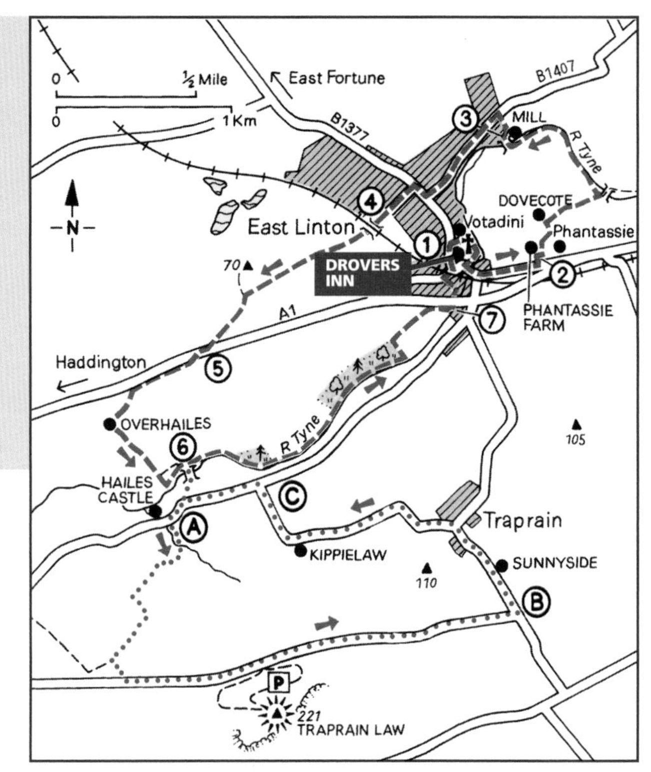

46: Through poppy fields from East Linton

This is a walk that is enjoyable at any time of year – but it's particularly lovely in summer when wild flowers line the way.

If you were to design your ideal walk, what would it include? A dash of history; a crumbling castle; perhaps some fields of waving corn and a peaceful riverbank? And maybe a pretty village, in which to settle down finally with a plate of good food? Well, this walk's for you then. It takes you on a lovely varied route through the fertile countryside of East Lothian, just a few miles outside Edinburgh.

The first part of the walk takes you past an old doo'cot (dovecote) where pigeons were bred for food. It once belonged to Phantassie house, a local property which was the birthplace of Sir John Rennie in 1761. Rennie was a civil engineer who, after studying at Edinburgh University, moved to London. There he constructed Southwark and Waterloo bridges, as well as designing dockyards, bridges and canals throughout the country.

Not far from the doo'cot is the extremely photogenic Preston Mill, which is owned by the National Trust for Scotland. This 18th-century grain mill was used to process the produce of East Lothian's fertile arable fields. It has a distinctive conical kiln, which was used for drying the grain, and a barn where the grain was ground. The machinery is driven by a waterwheel.

Later on, as you make your way towards Hailes Castle, you might well see the scarlet heads of poppies waving in among the ripening crops. Sadly, this is a sight seen all too rarely these days, as intensive agriculture has virtually eliminated them from the fields around here, but it would once have been commonplace. Poppies have been a symbol of blood, harvest and regeneration for thousands of years, as they grow in fields of grain and will rapidly colonise disturbed ground – this was most graphically illustrated in World War I, and poppies have, of course, also become a symbol of remembrance of lives lost.

Poppies were the sacred plant of the Roman crop goddess Ceres (from whose name we get the word 'cereal'). The Romans used to decorate her statues with garlands of poppies and barley, and poppy seeds were offered up during rituals to ensure a good harvest. Poppy seeds mixed with grains of barley have also been found in Egyptian relics dating from 2500 BC.

In Britain it was once believed that picking poppies would provoke a storm and they were nicknamed 'thundercup', 'thunderflower' or 'lightnings'. Whatever you call them, they're a glorious and welcome sight.

Walk directions

❶ From the Market Cross in the centre of the town, take the path that runs to the left of the church. When you come to the main street (the **Drovers Inn** is just here) bear left, then walk over the bridge and continue until you reach a garage on the right-hand side. Turn left here into the farm opposite the garage, following the sign for Houston Mill and Mill House.

❷ Follow the path round the farm buildings until you see the old doo'cot ahead of you. Turn right just in front of it and follow the path along the edge of the field. When you reach the footbridge, turn left to continue walking around the edge of the field, with the river on your right-hand side. At the next footbridge, cross over and go through the metal gate.

❸ Take the right-hand path across the field and go through the kissing gate to reach the old mill. Once you've inspected the mill – you can go inside when it's open – continue on to meet the main road, then turn left to walk back into the town. Turn right to walk along the High Street, then cross over the road and turn left to go down Langside.

❹ When you reach the recreation ground, maintain direction and walk towards the railway. Go through the underpass and walk ahead through the fields. Continue in the same direction, crossing over three walls with the help of some steps and two stiles. After you cross the third wall the track starts to become indistinct, but maintain direction until you reach a wooden sign. Turn left here to reach the road.

While there

The Museum of Flight at East Fortune, near Haddington, is Scotland's national museum of aviation. You can see wartime memorabilia and lots of old aircraft, including a Tigermoth, all housed in old World War II Nissen huts and hangers. Haddington itself is a prosperous town and was the birthplace in around 1513 of John Knox, the founder of the Presbyterian Church.

Look for

Hailes Castle, the ruins of which you'll see down by the River Tyne, dates back to the 13th century. It was one of the places where Mary, Queen of Scots, stayed when she and her lover Bothwell were fleeing from their enemies. The castle was eventually destroyed by Cromwell in 1650.

❺ Turn right, then cross over with care at the parking place to continue along the track running parallel to the road. Walk to Overhailes farm, through the yard, then bear left and follow the wide track down to Hailes Castle. Ignore the first path that joins from the left and go a few paces further to turn left along another path that leads to a bridge. (The extension to Traprain Law starts here.)

❻ Don't cross over the bridge but instead follow the track that runs to the left of the steps. You're now walking along the river's edge on a narrow path. Follow the path to cross a stile, walk along a field margin, then enter some woods. Walk up a flight of stairs, then down some steps, and continue following the path to walk under the road bridge.

❼ The path now runs through a garden and onto the road, where you turn right. Walk under the railway bridge, then turn left and return to the starting point of the walk in the town.

Drovers Inn

5 Bridge St, East Linton
EH40 3AG
Tel: 01620 860298
Directions: *5 miles (8km) east of Haddington, turn off the A1 and follow the road under the railway bridge; turn left*
Open: *11.30–11 (Thu–Sat 11.30–1)*
Bar meals: *lunch served all week, 11.30–2; dinner served Sun–Fri, 6–9.30; average main course £10*
Restaurant: *lunch and dinner served all week, 11.30–2, 6–9.30; average 3 course à la carte £25.50*
Brewery/company: *free house*
Principal beers: *Adnams Broadside, Deuchars IPA, Old Speckled Hen, Burton Real Ale*
Children welcome

Herdsmen used to *stop here as they drove their livestock to market. Those passing through in the late 19th century would undoubtedly have been aware of the then landlord's son's liking for young Jessie Cowe, daughter of the appropriately named local butcher. The church clock tower in the village square was named 'Jessie' after her. Those old drovers are long gone but the bar, with wooden floors, beamed ceilings and half-panelled walls, retains an old-world charm. Upstairs, though, is more sumptuous with rich colours, low-beamed ceilings and antique furniture.*

Bistro menus offer Highland haggis with a creamy pepper sauce, shank of Borders lamb with vegetables, and crispy-skinned codling on a basil and mustard mash. The chef's daily creations depend on seasonal local produce, while sizzling honey and ginger pie, chargrilled steaks and goats' cheese-filled patties with slow-roasted plum tomatoes are always popular.

Extension to Traprain Law

At Point ❻ on the main route, cross the bridge over the river and walk up the gravel track – it can get overgrown in summer with nettles and brambles. Continue following the path, bearing right along the road. When you reach Hailes Castle on the right-hand side, take the turning opposite on the left – Point Ⓐ.

Go through the green metal gate and follow the path as it bears right and becomes an enclosed track, with a wall on the left-hand side. Walk until you reach a gate saying 'farm road only', and take the turning on the left. Continue, to go through a gate and join the road, where you turn left. It's a bit of a long tramp now along the road and, though it's not too busy, do watch for cars. Eventually you'll reach Traprain Law on the right-hand side.

To enjoy the views, make a detour to climb the hill, which you reach via a stile. It was the site of a prehistoric hill fort. In 1919 a deep pit was discovered on the law, filled with an extraordinary collection of 4th-century silver plate, which had been crushed into pieces as if it was going to be melted down. Some think that it had been hidden there by Angle or Saxon thieves, early in the 5th century AD.

Otherwise continue along the road, pass the car park on the right-hand side and walk to the junction – Point Ⓑ. Turn left here, walk up past Sunnyside house, then turn left following the sign to Kippielaw. Continue on this quiet tarmac road, pass Kippielaw house, then follow the road as it bears right and goes downhill. At the bottom of the hill, Point Ⓒ, turn left and walk back towards Hailes Castle. Turn right in front of the castle, walk back over the footbridge, then turn sharp right, almost doubling back on yourself to walk along the river and rejoin the main route at Point ❻.

47: A stroll by Edinburgh's canal

An interesting linear walk provides an insight into the history and development of Edinburgh's Union Canal, which was built between 1818 and 1822.

Extending for 30 miles (48.2km), the canal meets the Forth and Clyde Canal at Falkirk, now marked by the great boat lift known as the Falkirk Wheel. Various seats beside the towpath enable you to rest and savour the scene.

Walk directions

❶ Begin the walk at the picnic site next to the canal bridge in Baird Road, noting the information board which tells you about the area. Turn left and follow the Union Canal towpath towards Edinburgh, passing rows of moored narrow boats. The land behind them represents the site of the old village gasworks, earmarked for development. Keep ahead to what is known as the 'betwixt and between stone', which marks the end of the fare stage for those travelling by barge from Edinburgh.

❷ Look out for a doo'cote (dovecote) over to your right. Constructed in 1713 for nearby Ratho House, the dovecote has

Walk information

Distance: 2 miles (3.2km)
Map: OS Explorer 350 Edinburgh
Start/finish: canal bridge, Baird Rd, Ratho; grid ref NT 139709
Ascent/gradient: negligible
Paths: canal towpath
Landscape: semi-residential

A brightly painted canal boat

boxes for more than a thousand birds. There is also an icehouse nearby, covered by thick undergrowth. Ratho House was rebuilt in the 1800s and rented by Corstorphine Golf Club in 1928. The club eventually acquired the house and later changed its name to Ratho Park Golf Club.

❸ As the canal bends to the right, the rooftops of Edinburgh edge into view. Look out, too, for the castellated roof of Ashley House. Approaching the next bridge, you pass a milestone with 24/7 inscribed on it – this represents 24 miles (38.4km) to Falkirk and 7 miles (11.2km) to Edinburgh Canal Basin. Pass another milestone to reach Gogar Moor Bridge. At this point retrace your steps back to the car park, completing the walk with a well-earned visit to the popular **Bridge Inn.**

Stylish barge-ware

Bridge Inn

27 Baird Rd, Ratho EH28 8RA
Tel: 0131 333 1320
Directions: *from Newbridge interchange B7030, follow signs for Ratho*
Open: *12–11 (Sat 11–12, Sun 12.30–11)*
Bar meals: *meals served all week, 12–9; average main course £6.95*
Restaurant: *lunch and dinner served all week, 12–2, 6.30–9; average 3 course à la carte £22*
Brewery/company: *free house*
Principal beers: *Bellhaven 80/-, Bellhaven Best*
Children welcome
Parking: *60*

Dating back to *about 1750, the Bridge Inn began life as a farmhouse before becoming a staging-post during the construction of the Union Canal in 1822. By the mid-1820s numerous canal travellers stopped here for refreshment. With a door at either end of the inn, a thirsty boatman could leave his horse walking along the towpath, enter by one door, down a pint of ale and exit by the other in time to meet his plodding steed. The pub was restored during the 1970s and is now thriving at the heart of the city's Canal Centre, well known for its fleet of restaurant boats and sightseeing launches.*

Local produce, freshly prepared and served, is the Bridge Inn's hallmark, and it has specialised in top quality Scottish meat for over 30 years. Typical dishes on the imaginative menu are venison casserole, pumpkin and pancetta risotto, stuffed roast pepper with lemon and mint couscous, grilled salmon fillet stuffed with haggis and served with raspberry and bramble butter, and haddock in batter or breadcrumbs.

48: Discovering Neptune's Staircase

The first survey for a coast-to-coast canal across Scotland, linking the lochs of the Great Glen, was made by James Watt, inventor of the steam engine, back in 1767.

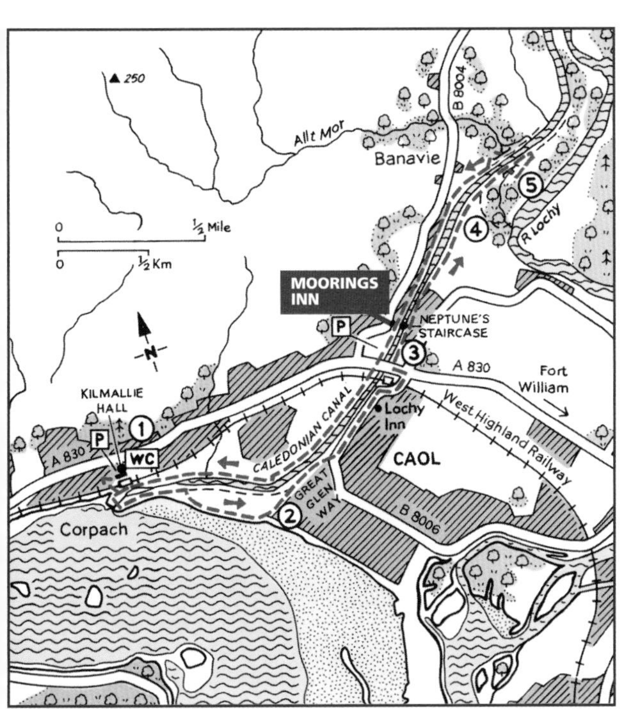

The Commissioners of Forfeited Estates had their hands on much of the land, and the canal fitted into their plans for civilising the Highlands and bringing them into the industrialised world.

But it was the economic and military necessities of the Napoleonic War that finally sent the men with the wheelbarrows up to Fort William in 1803. Despite the fact that nature had already provided 38 miles (61km) of the route, the canal was still a tremendous feat of civil engineering. Each of the 29 locks was designed to accommodate the width and length of a 40-gun frigate of Lord Nelson's navy. Four aqueducts let streams and rivers pass below the waterway, and there was a dam on Loch Lochy and diversion of the rivers Oich and Lochy. Loch Oich needed to be deepened, and for this task a steam dredger had to be not just built, but invented and designed. And before a single turf was shifted, the first essential, a brewery was required to supply the thousands of thirsty navvies.

For this great enterprise, only one man would do: Thomas Telford (1757–1834). However, even Telford's masonry crumbles eventually, and after falling into a state of neglect in the 20th century, the canal was on the verge of closure when, in 1996, the government promised £20 million for a complete refurbishment. The towpath has also been resurfaced as a cycleway, with a new National Trail, the Great Glen Way, running parallel.

Walk information

Distance: 4½ miles (7.2km)
Map: OS Explorer 392 Ben Nevis & Fort William
Start/finish: Kilmallie Hall, Corpach; grid ref NN 097768
Ascent/gradient: 2
Paths: wide towpaths
Landscape: banks of wide canal, shore of tidal loch

Walk directions

❶ Go down past Corpach Station to the canal and cross the sea lock that separates salt water from fresh water. Follow the canal (on your left) up past another lock, where a path on the right has a blue footpath sign and a Great Glen Way marker. It passes under tall sycamores to the shore. Follow the shoreline path past a football pitch and then turn left, across damp grass to a road sign that warns motorists of a nearby playground. A path ahead leads up a wooded bank to the towpath.

❷ Turn right along the towpath, for ½ mile (800m). Just before the Banavie swing bridge, a path down to the right has a Great Glen Way marker. Follow waymarkers on street signs to a level crossing, then turn left towards the other swing bridge, the one with the road on it.

❸ Just before the bridge, turn right at signs for the Great Glen Way and the Great Glen Cycle Route and continue along the towpath to Neptune's Staircase (the **Moorings Hotel** on the opposite bank is encountered on the return route). The fanciful name was given to the group of eight locks by Thomas Telford himself. It takes about 90 minutes for boats to work through the system. As each lock fills, slow boiling currents come up from underneath, like bath water emptying but in reverse.

❹ A gate marks the top of the locks. About 200 yards (183m) later, a grey gate on the right leads to a dump for dead cars; ignore this one. Over the next 100 yards (91m) the canal crosses a little wooded valley, with a black fence on the right. Now comes a second grey gate. Go through, to a track turning back sharp right and descending to ford a small stream.

❺ On the right, the stream passes right under the canal in an arched tunnel, and alongside is a second tunnel which provides a walkers' way to the other side. Water from the canal drips into the tunnel – try not to think of the large boats sailing directly over your head! At the tunnel's end, a track runs up to join the canal's northern towpath. Turn right, back down the towpath. After passing the **Moorings Hotel** by Neptune's Staircase, cross the A830 to a level crossing without warning lights. Continue along the right-hand towpath. After a mile (1.6km) the towpath track leads back to the Corpach double lock.

Moorings Hotel

Banavie, Fort William PH33 7LY
Tel: 01397 772797
Directions: *from the A82 in Fort William follow signs for Mallaig, then turn left onto the A830 for 1 mile (1.6km); cross the canal bridge then take the first right, signed to Banavie*
Open: *12–11.45*
Bar meals: *food served all week, 12–9.30; average main course £7.95*
Restaurant: *dinner served all week, 7–9.30; average 4 course fixed price £26*
Brewery/company: *free house*
Principal beers: *Calders 70/-, Sport*
Children welcome
Dogs allowed
Parking: *80*
Rooms: *28 bedrooms en suite from s£40, d£80*

The Moorings stands *on the bank of the Caledonian Canal beside Neptune's Staircase – a flight of eight locks that raise boats by 64 feet (21m). This striking modern hotel has panoramic views on clear days towards Ben Nevis and the surrounding mountains. Most bedrooms share this stunning outlook, including a new wing that mirrors the shape of the nearby Thomas Telford house. The Upper Deck lounge and popular Mariners' Bar share the nautical theme, and offer an appealing place for a drink or a meal.*

The daily changing bar food has a strong inclination towards local fish such as West Coast haddock and loch salmon, as well as Angus beef, Grampian chicken, and haggis served with clapshot and Drambuie sauce. Herb-roast rack of lamb, pan-seared scallops on wilted spinach, and gently baked filled of hake make up the numbers, along with bangers, burgers and, of course, a range of sandwiches.

While there

Much to Telford's distress, the canal was a loss-making enterprise from the day it opened. One reason was the coming of the railways. At Banavie, the West Highland Railway is Britain's most beautiful. During the summer, the steam-powered Jacobite Steam Train runs daily to Mallaig and back.

Look for

From Fort William, Britain's biggest hill appears as a mere hump. The canalside, however, gives the best view into the great Northern Corrie of Ben Nevis. On its right-hand side, ranged one behind the other, rise the buttresses of the country's largest crag. Across the back runs a narrow edge of granite, linking it to the neighbouring Carn Mor Dearg.

49: A scenic route around Plockton

Suitable for families and more ardent hikers, this varied forest walk offers great views towards Skye , one of Scotland's most romantic locations, before passing alongside scenic Loch Lundie.

Walk information

Distance: 5 miles (8 km)
Map: OS Explorer 428 Applecross
Start/finish: Plockton Hotel, Plockton; grid ref NG 803334
Ascent/gradient: 2
Paths: mainly paths and roads
Landscape: forest and loch

The shoreline at Plockton

Walk directions

❶ On leaving the **Plockton Hotel,** take the main road out of the village and cross the railway bridge. The road can be busy but there is sufficient verge to walk alongside it. Continue over a road junction, cross a small bridge and keep ahead up the hill. Look to the right for superb views of the Isle of Skye and Applecross.

❷ At the next junction turn left towards Strome and Duncraig. Once over the cattle grid look out for a wooden post on the right directing you to the footpath to Achnandarach. Cross the burn (stream) by the stepping stones and follow the path. In spring this stretch of the walk dazzles with carpets of primroses and large yellow globe flowers.

❸ Keep ahead along a tree-lined

Plockton Hotel

Harbour St, Plockton IV52 8TN
Tel: 01599 544274
Directions: on A87 to Kyle of Lochalsh turn off at Balcamara; Plockton is 7 miles (11.2km) north
Open 11–11.45 (Sun 12.30–11)
Bar meals: lunch and dinner served all week, 12–2.15, 6–9.15; average main course £9
Restaurant: lunch and dinner served all week, 12–2.15, 6–9.15; average 3 course à la carte £17
Brewery/company: free house
Principal beers: Caledonian Deuchars IPA
Children welcome
Rooms: 15 bedrooms en suite from s£40, d£60

***Plockton stretches along** the shores of Loch Carron, looking towards the Applecross mountains, and it is hard to imagine a more lovely spot for a hotel. It was built in 1827 as a private house, and recent developments have resulted in a new garden restaurant and a few more pretty bedrooms in a nearby cottage annexe. The atmosphere is relaxed and friendly.*

The hotel has built its reputation around food, and was awarded the accolade of Scotland's AA Seafood Pub of the Year 2004. Local produce takes pride of place on the menu, and locally caught fish and shellfish are prepared in the purpose-built smokehouse behind the hotel. Lunchtime sees a range of freshly made snacks, from sandwiches and jacket potatoes to mussels in white wine, a seafood platter from the smokery, haggis with clapshot, or perhaps Plockton prawns. In the evening the choice increases to take in skate wing in black butter, queen scallops with bacon, garlic and cream, and Moroccan lamb casserole.

path cutting through the forest. Once clear of the woodland, look out for two houses, one of which is designed in the Japanese style. At this junction turn left and walk down through the small village of Achnandarach and back to the main road.

❹ On reaching the post box, turn right and follow the road beside picturesque Loch Lundie. At certain times of the year you may catch sight of herons and other bird life on the water. At the next junction follow the signs for Strome, and then look for a gate and post indicating one mile. Take this well maintained path beside the railway line and follow it back to Plockton.

❺ Pass beneath a small railway bridge, and immediately beyond it look out for spectacular views of Plockton and Loch Carron. Turn right at the end of the path and go downhill, back into the village to return to the **Plockton Hotel.**

Loch Carron from Plockton

50: Craigower, a spectacular Perthshire viewpoint

Perthshire is great for walking, and this invigorating linear route captures the beauty and character of this magical landscape.

Rising to the north of Pitlochry is the rocky outcrop of Craigower. This hill, at one time used as a beacon, is now in the care of the National Trust for Scotland who permit access to the summit.

Its superb setting provides splendid views over the confluence of the rivers Tummel and Garry to the north and west, and the valleys of the Tummel and Tay to the south-east.

At the summit of Craigower, there is an annotated photograph which highlights important landmarks in the area, especially the view to the west, which stretches as far as Glencoe.

Walk directions

❶ Turn left on leaving the **Moulin Hotel,** following the road signposted to Craigower. Head for the golf course – and make sure no-one is playing before you cross it. Continue past a small cottage and on, up into some conifer woods on the lower slopes of Craigower.

❷ The route through these woods is clearly signposted and should present no real difficulties, although please remember to bear left when crossing the forestry road in order to stay on the direct route to the summit.

❸ Near the top this route becomes steep, but if you wish to avoid the steep ascent, there is an alternative. Simply turn right and stay on the forestry road for a longer, more gradual approach to the summit. This road can also be used as an alternative return route.

❹ Retrace your steps back down to the **Moulin Hotel.**

Walk information

Distance: 3 miles (4.8 km)
Map: OS Explorer 21 Pitlochry & Loch Tummel
Start/finish: Moulin Hotel, Moulin; grid ref NN 944593
Ascent/gradient: 3
Paths: forest roads and paths, some steep
Landscape: tree-clad slopes

The hydro-electric dam at Pitlochry

Moulin Hotel

11–13 Kirkmichael Rd, Moulin, Pitlochry PH16 5EW
Tel: 01796 472196
Directions: *from the A9 at Pitlochry take the A923; Moulin is ¾ mile (1.2km) further on*
Open: *12–11 (Fri–Sat 12–11.45)*
Bar meals: *food served all week, 12–9.30; average main course £6.95*
Restaurant: *dinner served all week, 6–9*
Brewery/company: *free house*
Principal beers: *Moulin Braveheart, Old Remedial, Ale of Atholl, Moulin Light*
Children welcome
Dogs allowed
Parking: *40*
Rooms: *15 bedrooms en suite from s£40, d£50*

Half a century *before the Jacobite rebellion of 1745, the Moulin Hotel was established at the foot of Ben Vrakie (2,757 feet/827m), on the old drove road from Dunkeld to Kingussie. The modern road runs through nearby Pitlochry, leaving Moulin as an ideal base for walking and touring. The large, white-painted pub with its summer courtyard garden is popular with tourists and locals alike. In winter, two blazing log fires set the scene for a game of cards, dominoes or bar billiards.*

Well-kept real ales come from the pub's own micro-brewery, and there's plenty of Gaelic fare on the big all-day menu. Start with potted hough and oatcakes, or Skye mussels with garlic, before moving on to venison Braveheart, haggis and neeps, or a game casserole McDuff. There's haddock or salmon too, and vegetarians can expect sautéed mushroom pancakes, stuffed peppers, and vegetable goulash.

Bedrooms in the hotel vary in size and style.

Walking in safety

All these walks are suitable for any reasonably fit person. Route finding is usually straightforward but, as mentioned previously, you should carry the relevant Ordnance Survey map in addition to the route and walk description.

Risks

Although each walk has been researched with a view to minimising the risks to the walkers who follow its route, no walk in the countryside can be considered to be completely free from risk. Walking in the outdoors will always require a degree of common sense and judgement to ensure that it is as safe as possible.

- Be particularly careful on cliff paths and in upland terrain, where the consequences of a slip can be very serious.
- Remember to check tidal conditions before walking along the seashore.
- Some sections of route are by, or cross roads. Take care and remember traffic is a danger even on minor country lanes.
- Be careful around farmyard machinery and livestock, especially if you have children or a dog with you.
- Be aware of the consequences of changes of weather and check the forecast before you set off. Carry spare clothing and a torch if you are walking in the winter months. Remember that the weather can change very quickly at any time of the year, and in moorland and heathland areas, mist and fog can make route finding much harder. Don't set out in these conditions unless you are confident of your navigation skills in poor visibility. In summer remember to take account of the heat and sun; wear a hat and carry spare water.
- On walks away from centres of population you should carry a whistle and survival bag. If you do have an accident requiring the emergency services, make a note of your position as accurately as possible and dial 999.

Acknowledgements

The following photographs are held in the Automobile Association's own photo library (AA PHOTO LIBRARY) and were taken by the following photographers:

Front Cover: J Miller; 3, M Birkitt; 8/9, A Lawson; 10, R Moss; 16, P Baker; 18, H Williams; 21, H Williams; 26, S&O Matthews; 31, S&O Matthews; 35, D Forss; 38, T Souter; 40, D Croucher; 42, S&O Matthews; 45, M Birkitt; 50, W Voysey; 52, A Molyneux; 54, H Williams; 58, S Day; 61, S Day; 70, V Greaves; 75, D Forss; 76, H Burns; 78, M Birkitt; 85, S&O Matthews; 90, E Bowness; 92, S Day; 97, D Tarn; 99, M Birkitt; 102, C Lees; 106, S&O Matthews; 109, D Tarn; 117, D Croucher; 119, W Voysey; 120, W Voysey; 124, H Williams; 125, R Weir: 127, R Moss.